The EVERYTHING KIDS'
Fun with Food
Placemats
FUN AND GAMES

Puzzles, games, jokes, and more for tons of mealtime fun!

Use at home—or on the go!

Adams media
Avon, Massachusetts

An Everything® Series product.
Everything® and everything.com® are registered trademarks of
F+W Media, Inc.

Published by Adams Media,
a division of F+W Media, Inc.
57 Littlefield Street
Avon, MA 02322. U.S.A.
www.adamsmedia.com

Contains material adapted and abridged from *The Everything®
KIDS' Animal Puzzle and Activity Book* by Beth L. Blair and Jennifer A.
Ericsson, copyright © 2005 by F+W Media, Inc., ISBN 10: 1-59337-305-
8, ISBN 13: 978-1-59337-305-4; *The Everything® KIDS' Astronomy Book* by
Kathi Wagner and Sheryl Racine, copyright © 2008 by F+W Media,
Inc., ISBN 10: 1-59869-544-4, ISBN 13: 978-1-59869-544-1; *The Everything® KIDS' Bugs Book* by Kathi Wagner, copyright © 2003 by F+W
Media, Inc., ISBN 10: 1-58062-892-3, ISBN 13: 978-1-58062-892-1; *The
Everything® KIDS' Cars and Trucks Puzzle and Activity* by Charles Timmerman, copyright © 2006 by F+W Media, Inc., ISBN 10: 1-59337-
703-7, ISBN 13: 978-1-59337-703-8; *The Everything® KIDS' Crazy Puzzles*
by Beth L. Blair and Jennifer A. Ericsson, copyright © 2005 by F+W
Media, Inc., ISBN 10: 1-59337-361-9, ISBN 13: 978-1-59337-361-0; *The
Everything® KIDS' Dinosaurs Book* by Kathi Wagner and Sheryl Racine,
copyright © 2005 by F+W Media, Inc., ISBN 10: 1-59337-360-0, ISBN
13: 978-1-59337-360-3; *The Everything® KIDS' Dragons Puzzle and Activity Book* by Scot Ritchie, copyright © 2008 by F+W Media, Inc., ISBN
10: 1-59869-623-8, ISBN 13: 978-1-59869-623-3; *The Everything® KIDS'
Environment Book* by Sheri Amsel, copyright © 2007 by F+W Media,
Inc., ISBN 10: 1-59869-670-X, ISBN 13: 978-1-59869-670-7; *The Everything® KIDS' Fairies Puzzle and Activity Book* by Charles Timmerman,
copyright © 2007 by F+W Media, Inc., ISBN 10: 1-59869-394-8, ISBN
13: 978-1-59869-394-2; *The Everything® KIDS' Joke Book* by Michael
Dahl, copyright © 2002 by F+W Media, Inc., ISBN 10: 1-58062-686-6,
ISBN 13: 978-1-58062-686-6; *The Everything® KIDS' Knock Knock Book*
by Aileen Weintraub, copyright © 2004 by F+W Media, Inc., ISBN
10: 1-59337-127-6, ISBN 13: 978-1-59337-127-2; *The Everything® KIDS'
More Puzzles Book* by Scot Ritchie, copyright © 2010 by F+W Media,
Inc., ISBN 10: 1-4405-0647-7, ISBN 13: 978-1-4405-0647-5; *The Everything® KIDS' More Word Searches Puzzle and Activity Book* by Beth L.
Blair and Jennifer Ericsson, copyright © 2010 by F+W Media, Inc.,
ISBN 10: 1-4405-0562-4, ISBN 13: 978-1-4405-0562-1; *The Everything®
KIDS' Nature Book* by Kathiann M. Kowalski, copyright © 2002 by
F+W Media, Inc., ISBN 10: 1-58062-684-X, ISBN 13: 978-1-58062-684-
2; *The Everything® KIDS' Pirates Puzzle and Activity Book* by Beth L. Blair
and Jennifer Ericsson, copyright © 2006 by F+W Media, Inc., ISBN
10: 1-59337-607-3, ISBN 13: 978-1-59337-607-9; *The Everything® KIDS'
Princess Puzzle and Activity Book* by Charles Timmerman and Calla
Timmerman, copyright © 2006 by F+W Media, Inc., ISBN 10: 1-59337-
704-5, ISBN 13: 978-1-59337-704-5; *The Everything® KIDS' Racecars Puzzle and Activity Book* by Beth L. Blair and Jennifer Ericsson, copyright
© 2008 by F+W Media, Inc., ISBN 10: 1-59869-243-7 ISBN 13: 978-1-
59869-243-3; *The Everything® KIDS' Riddles and Brain Teasers Book* by
Kathi Wagner and Audrey Wagner, copyright © 2004 by F+W Media,
Inc., ISBN 10: 1-59337-036-9, ISBN 13: 978-1-59337-036-7; *The Everything® KIDS' Sharks Book* by Kathi Wagner and Obe Wagner, copyright
© 2005 by F+W Media, Inc., ISBN 10: 1-59337-304-X, ISBN 13: 978-1-
59337-304-7; *The Everything® KIDS' Travel Activity Book* by Eric Hanson
and Jeanne Hanson, copyright © 2002 by F+W Media, Inc., ISBN 10:
1-58062-641-6, ISBN 13: 978-1-58062-641-5.

ISBN 10: 1-4405-2883-7
ISBN 13: 978-1-4405-2883-5

Printed by RR Donnelley, Shenzhen, China.
10 9 8 7 6 5 4 3 2 1
June 2011

*This product is available at quantity discounts for bulk purchases.
For information, please call 1-800-289-0963.*

THINK GREEN!

One Piece at a Time

Protecting the earth from pollution can seem like a job that is too big. But if each person starts to do just one or two things to help out, soon the problem will be much smaller! Break the Letter Shift Code (A=B, B=C, C=D, etc.) to learn an important thought to keep in mind!

S-Z-J-D   B-Z-Q-D

N-E   S-G-D

D-Z-Q-S-G.

X-N-T   B-Z-M'S

K-H-U-D

V-H-S-G-N-T-S

H-S!

Sign of the Times

Connect the dots to find a familiar and important symbol. Use your markers or crayons to color it in!

Did You Know?

A Runny Nose Costs Trees

If every home in the United States bought one box of 100-percent recycled tissues, we could save more than 87,000 trees! We could also stop more than 300 garbage trucks full of trash (in tissues) from going to the landfills.

Daffy Definition

Fill in the shapes that contain the letters T-R-A-S-H to get the silly answer to this question: What do you call three feet of trash?

Dump Not!

Find words from the list in the dump. Use a colored marker to highlight these items. They don't need to be dumped — they can be recycled and reused! Hint: Words can be up, down, backwards, or diagonal.

STEEL	PLASTIC	MAGAZINES
PAPER	SODA CANS	ALUMINUM
CLOTH	MILK JUGS	MOTOR OIL
GLASS	CARDBOARD	CAR BATTERIES

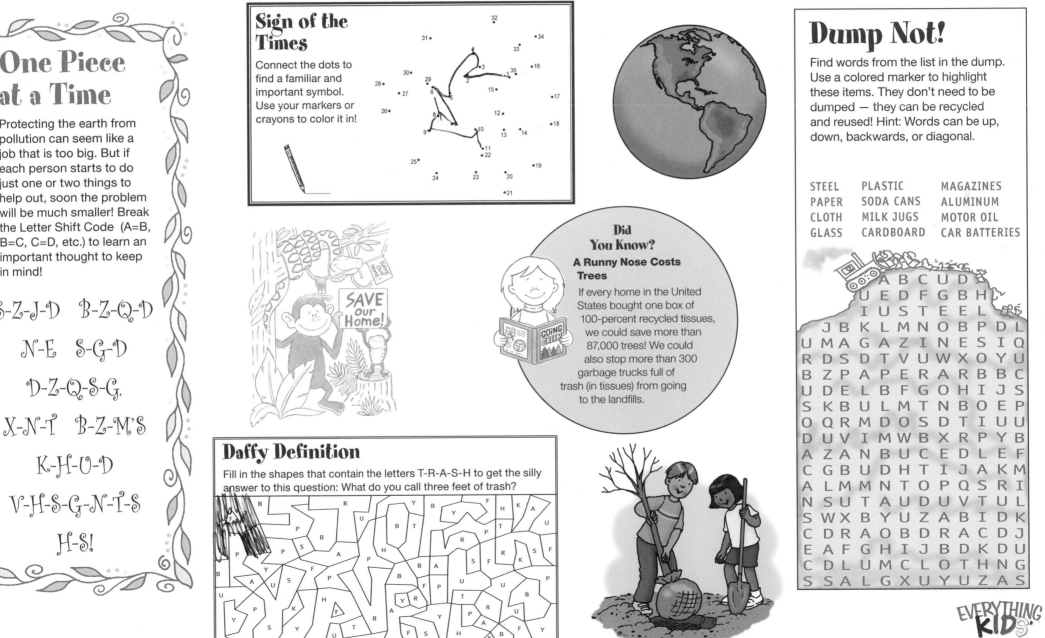

SAVE our Home!

GOING GREEN

ANSWERS

One Piece at a Time

T-A-K-E C-A-R-E
O-F T-H-E
E-A-R-T-H.
Y-O-U C-A-N'T
L-I-V-E
W-I-T-H-O-U-T
I-T!

Dump Not!

Sign of the Times

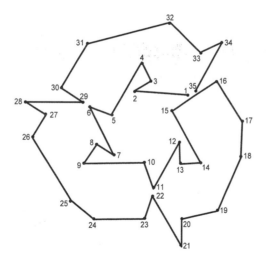

Daffy Definition

A JUNK YARD

Animal Fun

Playing in the Mud

Grassland animals like the hippo, rhino, and elephant like to roll in the mud and get all dirty. Why? Each of the letters in a column belongs in one of the boxes directly below it. When you fit all the letters in the proper boxes, you will be able to read what mud does for these animals. Some letters are already done for you!

HINT: Black boxes are the spaces between words.

Drew, I want you to go out and get nice and dirty today!

Aw, mom! Do I have to?

Island Attraction

Galapagos tortoises, which can weigh more than 500 pounds each, were once hunted for their meat and oil. Now they are protected by law. Follow the directions in this tortoise's shell. When you are done, you will know which humans, and their vacation dollars, have become very helpful in protecting these turtles!

TORTOISE

- move second T to end
- change first O to U
- move O before U
- delete E

Sounds Like . . .

How many pet sounds can you make from the letters listed below? Letters can be used more than once, but notice that not all the letters in the alphabet are available to you. Even so, we bet you can make at least ten noisy words.

A B E G H I K L M
O P Q U R S T W Y

1. _____
2. _____
3. _____
4. _____
5. _____
6. _____
7. _____
8. _____
9. _____
10. _____

I collect acorns and bury them for cold weather. The problem is, I always forget where I've left them. Sometimes the acorns stay where I left them and grow into trees. I may be gray or black and I've got a bushy tail that makes me irresistible. **What am I?**

What am I?

A squirrel

Knock knock!
Who's there?
Beagle.
Beagle who?
Beagle with lox!

Knock knock!
Who's there?
Feline.
Feline who?
Feline fine, and you?

Perfect Parakeet

There are many parakeets in this cage, but Andrew wants one in particular. Find the bird that has all the following:

- white body
- dark wing
- long tail
- 3 spots near beak
- 3 stripes on forehead

ANSWERS

Playing in the Mud

MUD IS ANIMAL SUNSCREEN! IT PROTECTS THEIR SKIN AND KEEPS IT MOIST.

Sounds Like . . .

bark, growl, meow, purr, squeak, squeal, tweet, whistle, yelp, yowl

Perfect Parakeet

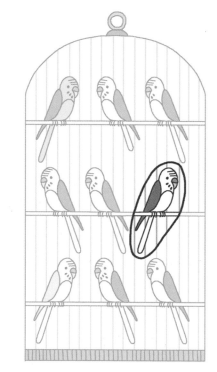

Island Attraction

TORTOISE

TOROISET
move second T to end

TUROISET
change first O to U

TOURISET
move O before U

TOURIST
delete E

Tough Trucks

Gravel Movers

These two dumptrucks hold exactly 3 tons and 5 tons of gravel. You need to haul 4 tons of gravel to the construction site. How can you measure the gravel without a scale? Hint: Gravel can be moved between the dumptrucks.

Mathemagical Roof

Roofer Ralph has put shingles on this house that he hauled with his truck. Now he needs your help to complete this roof. For each empty shingle (or box) below, enter the sum of the two numbers beneath it on either corner. One example is already done (5+1=6). Complete all of the shingles to the very top.

44

23 21

14   9   12

8   6   3   9

3   5   1   2   7

Farmer Joe

Farmer Joe is using his pickup truck to haul a fox, a goose, and a bag of grain from the woods to his barn. His truck can only haul one thing at a time. For obvious reasons, he can't leave the fox alone with the goose, or the goose with the grain. How does Farmer Joe get his cargo safely to his barn?

Letter Bulldozers

Using letters in the word BULLDOZERS, you can make the words RED and DOLL and many others. Can you find at least twenty words contained in BULLDOZERS?

1. _____	11. _____
2. _____	12. _____
3. _____	13. _____
4. _____	14. _____
5. _____	15. _____
6. _____	16. _____
7. _____	17. _____
8. _____	18. _____
9. _____	19. _____
10. _____	20. _____

ANSWERS

Gravel Movers

Here is a solution:
1. Fill up the 5-ton truck with gravel.
2. Pour gravel from the 5-ton truck into the 3-ton truck until it is full. The 5-ton truck will have 2 tons of gravel remaining.
3. Empty the 3-ton truck.
4. Pour the 2-tons of gravel from the 5-ton truck into the 3-ton truck.
5. Full up the 5-ton truck with gravel again.
6. Pour gravel from the 5-ton truck into the 3-ton truck until it is full. Since the 3-ton truck already had 2-tons in it, only 1-ton from the the 5-ton truck will be poured.

The 5-ton truck will now have the 4-tons of gravel needed at the construction site.

Mathemagical Roof

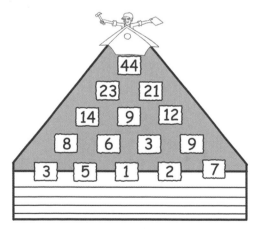

Farmer Joe

Farmer Joe hauls the goose to his barn, then returns to the woods. He hauls the fox to his barn and returns to the woods with the goose. He leaves the goose and hauls the grain to his barn. Farmer Joe returns to the woods and hauls the goose to his barn. Everything has been safely moved to Farmer Joe's barn.

Letter Bulldozers

Here are some words found in BULLDOZERS:

bed bell blue blur bold bored boulder bred bud bull bus do doe does doll dose double doze dub due duel dull duo lobe lore lose loser loud lube ode old or orb ore our red rob robe rod role roll rose rosebud rub rude rule sell sled slob slur so sod sold sour sub sue sure us use zero

You may have found others. More words can be made by adding letters to these words.

Fairyland

Flowers & Mushrooms

Draw two flowers and three mushrooms in the boxes below.
No flower should be next to another flower.
No mushroom should be next to another mushroom.

Flower Equations

Can you help the flower fairy figure out what numbers should go in the boxes to complete these equations?

=5   =20

-8   +19   =25

+6   +12   +61   +37

7   -73

Break the Spell

marriage apartment excede

rhyme arguemint grammar

surprise heroes ocassion

wierd maybe schedule

yeild calendar among

familiar balanse describe

height recieve ninety

control reccomend choose

Help this girl get back to her fairy godmother. Break the spell by crossing out the one misspelled word in each group. If you need to, use a dictionary to check the spellings.

Tooth Fairy Animal

Solve this puzzle to find out what animal takes the place of the tooth fairy in some countries.

1. The first letter is in **mother** but not **brother**.
2. The second letter is in **bowl** and **spoon**.
3. The third letter comes before **V W X**.
4. The fourth letter is in the middle of **himself**.
5. The fifth letter is the fifth in the alphabet.

<u>m</u> <u>o</u> <u>u</u> <u>s</u> <u>e</u>
 1   2   3   4   5

Fairyland Riddles

I'm found in the fairy forest
and I end with an E;
I provide plenty of shade,
and you can climb on me.
Draw a picture of what I am:

I'm red and I'm tasty
and I start with an A;
fairyland teachers love me,
and I keep the doctor away.
Draw a picture of what I am:

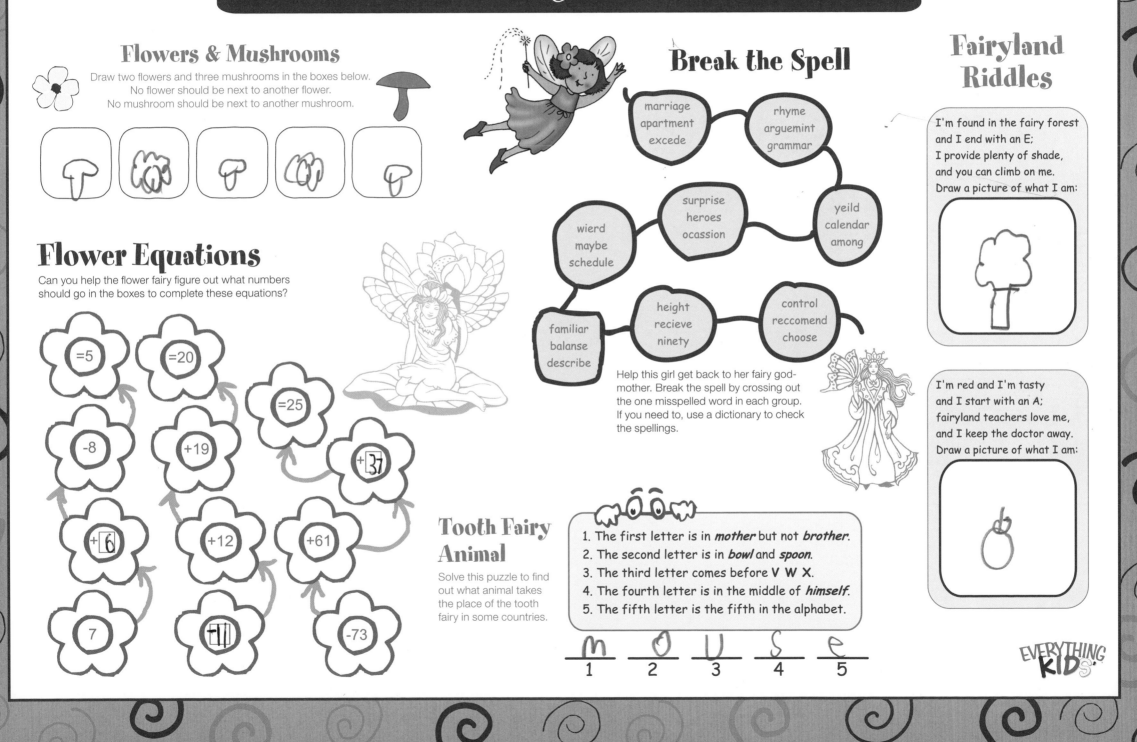

ANSWERS

Flowers & Mushrooms

Flower Equations

Break the Spell

marriage
apartment
~~exeede~~

rhyme
~~arguemint~~
grammar

surprise
heroes
~~ocassion~~

~~yeild~~
calendar
among

~~wierd~~
maybe
schedule

familiar
~~balanse~~
describe

height
~~recieve~~
ninety

control
~~reccomend~~
choose

Tooth Fairy Animal

$$\underline{\underset{1}{M}} \quad \underline{\underset{2}{O}} \quad \underline{\underset{3}{U}} \quad \underline{\underset{4}{S}} \quad \underline{\underset{5}{E}}$$

Fairyland Riddles

Tree

Apple

Under the Big Top

Tricky Trunk

This performer uses 11 props to create his circus act. Can you find them all? Only the first 2 letters of each word are provided!

BA—, BU—, CL—, SH—, HA—, HO—,
MA—, NO—, RU— CH—, WH—, CU—, WI—

```
W H O O P E E C U S H I O N
H A M A K E U P K W I G L B
O T J S H O E S N E S O N U
R U B B E R C H I C K E N L
N O O L L A B B U Z Z E R C
```

The Entertainers

Everyone enjoys watching a good performer! Highlight the names of 6 kinds of entertainers hiding in the stands beneath the acrobat.

Extra fun: Read the leftover letters from left to right and top to bottom to find the answer to this riddle: Why did the acrobat put a rabbit on his bald head?

MAGICIAN
STORYTELLER
VENTRILOQUIST
MUSICIAN
PUPPETEER
MIME

```
        V E
H   V   R E
E   E   E T
N   N   E E
S   T   T T
T   R   E P
O   I   P U
R   L   P P
Y   O   U E
T   Q   P I
E   U   E E
E D I M T H
D D L T E U
E H A R H E
P T R H E V
M U I E I U
N A C I G A M
```

Fun at the Fair

Sam, Pam, and Dan had a great time at the state fair! The kids want to try lots of fair foods—but where are their favorites? Read the big sign listing what's available, then find the tent that has that food inside.

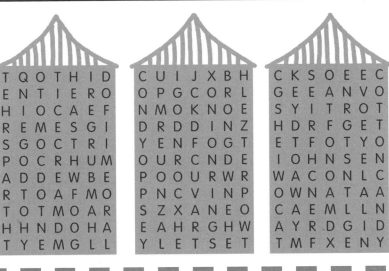

TACO...........2.00	SNO-CONE.......1.00	COTTON CANDY...1.00
GYROS.........3.00	SODA.............. .75	PRETZEL..............1.00
HOTDOG......1.25	CORN DOG.....2.25	HAMBURGER........2.00
ICE CREAM...1.00	FRENCH FRIES...2.00	ONION RINGS......2.00

```
T Q O T H I D       C U I J X B H       C K S O E E C
E N T I E R O       O P G C O R L       G E E A N V O
H I O C A E F       N M O K N O E       S Y I T R O T
R E M E S G I       D R D D I N Z       H D R F G E T
S G O C T R I       Y E N F O G T       E T F O T Y O
P O C R H U M       O U R C N D E       I O H N S E N
A D D E W B E       P O O U R W R       W A C O N L C
R T O A F M O       P N C V I N P       O W N A T A A
T O T M O A R       S Z X A N E O       C A E M L L N
H H N D O H A       E A H R G H W       A Y R D G I D
T Y E M G L L       Y L E T S E T       T M F X E N Y
```

When the **circus** comes to town Bobby always goes to see it. His favorite part is when the elephants build a pyramid. "Can you believe it?" asks the announcer. "A record **21 ELEPHANTS**!" Amazed, Bobby starts counting: 1 on top, 2 below it, 3 more below them, and so on. If the announcer is right, how many elephants will be on the **bottom** row?

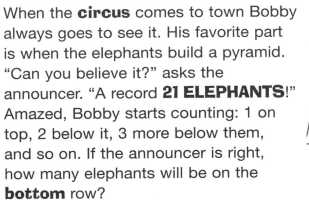

ANSWERS

Tricky Trunk

W H O O P E E C U S H I O N
H A M A K E U P K W I G L B
O T J S H O E S N E S O N U
R U B B E R C H I C K E N L
N O O L L A B B U Z Z E R C

The Entertainers

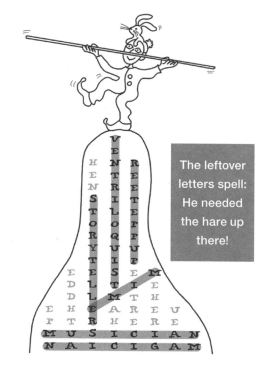

The leftover letters spell: He needed the hare up there!

Fun at the Fair

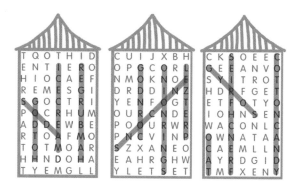

How many elephants on the bottom row?

6 elephants

Creepy Crawlies

Small Survivors

The desert is home to many small creatures who seem to survive there without much difficulty. There are five of these hidden in this word puzzle. To find them, take one letter from each column moving from left to right. Cross them off as you go—each letter can only be used once. The first creature has been done for you.

```
S O I T L T S
C P E U E T S
B E C D S E T
L E R C K R E
T R A M I E S
```

1. SPIDERS
2. _____
3. _____
4. _____
5. _____

Small But Deadly

This desert hunter stays sheltered during the day. At night it comes out looking for prey, which it injects with deadly venom. Fill in the blocks as directed to see this small but dangerous creature. Would you like to meet one?

- Find box 1 and copy the pattern into square 1.
- Find box 2 and copy the pattern into square 2.
- Continue doing this until you have copied all the boxes into the grid.

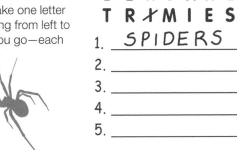

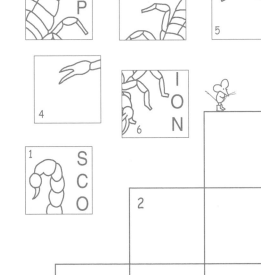

The New Bug in Town

Dr. Pheromone has discovered a new kind of moth. Use the clues below to figure out which of the moths pictured is the new one!

1. The new moth is in a column that has two beetles.

2. The new moth is in a row that has two other moths.

3. There is no moth directly to the right of the new moth.

HINT: Columns go up and down, and rows go side to side.

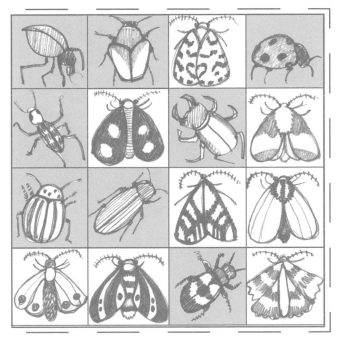

Strong as a Bug

of pounds you weigh: _____

Multiply by 850: _____

This is how many pounds you could lift if you were as strong as a rhinocerous beetle!

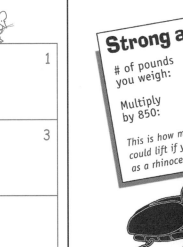

Super Bug

The rhinoceros beetle is about the size of a coffee mug. That's big for a bug! But more amazing than his size is his strength. This rainforest superstar can support 850 times his own weight! This makes it the strongest creature in the world. Stronger than an elephant? Yes—an elephant can only carry one quarter of his own weight!

Use the "Strong as a Bug" formula to figure out how many pounds you could lift if you were as strong as a rhinoceros beetle.

ANSWERS

Small Survivors

1. SPIDERS
2. CRICKET
3. BEETLES
4. LOCUSTS
5. TERMITE

Small But Deadly

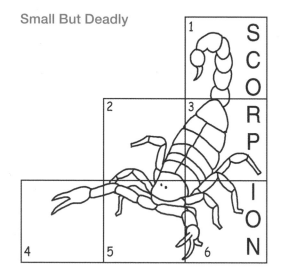

The New Bug in Town

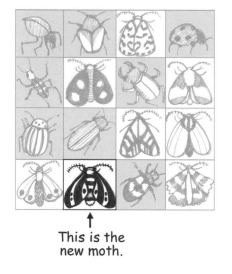

This is the new moth.

Super Bug

Of course, everyone's answer will be different depending on what they weigh. Let's try the formula assuming that you weigh 100 pounds. If you were as strong as a rhinoceros beetle, you could lift 85,000 pounds! That's forty-two and a half tons! Now, if you weighed 100 pounds, but were as strong as an elephant, you could lift only 25 pounds. That's the same as 5 bags of sugar. You can see that ounce for ounce the rhinoceros beetle deserves the title "strongest creature in the world"!!

Something Fishy

What part of a shark weighs the most?

The scales!

Let's Play

Use the decoder to figure out this riddle:

What's a shark's favorite game?

smack, yummy, gulp, urp, urp, slurp, yummy

yum, crunch, munch

urp, munch, gulp, gurgle, munch, crack

LET'S PLAY!

Let's not!

A = gulp
D = gurgle

E = munch
H = crunch

L = urp
O = slurp

R = crack
S = smack

T = yum
W = yummy

Funny Fish

Use the clues to fill in the spaces in all of the fish. The last letter of one answer is the first letter of the next answer. When you are done, place the numbered letters on the lines to answer the riddle!

1. Kind of lizard
2. Hooting bird
3. Not quiet
4. Can't hear
5. Short Friday
6. Creative thoughts
7. Opposite of north

What are the most expensive fish at the pet store?

___ ___ ___ ___ ___ ___ ___ ___
1. 2. 3. 4. 5. 6. 7. 8.

Under the Sea

BARRACUDA
CLAM
CRAB
DOLPHIN
DUGONG
EEL
FISH
JELLYFISH
KRILL
LOBSTER
MARLIN
NARWHAL
NAUTILUS
OCTOPUS
PORPOISE
SARDINE
SEAHORSE
SEAL
SEA LAMPREY
SEA TURTLE
SEA URCHIN
SHARK
SHRIMP
SKATE
SQUID
STARFISH
STINGRAY
SWORDFISH
TUNA
WHALE

More than two-thirds of the world is covered with water, and it is home to many, many creatures. Find the 30 that are listed here.

```
S T I N G R A Y K H S I F D R O W S
L P W S Q U I C R S K A T E S T I N
P O O E L O B R E O C L S Q U I A L
S H H R A S T A D A W O A V E L L Y
L S S N P R H B K S B B S R A A O U
U I I A D O A C L Q A S E H T E B L
E F E C R R I U O U R Q W T R S L Y
N R O S B D P S B I R R D I A I N E
S A E N A G I K E T A L O B R E M R
E T S E A N D N E N C R W K E D I P
L S Q T I U E S E A U R C H I N S M
T K U E D I T S Q U D U G O N G L A
R B R I F K N I W E A K S Q U L O L
U I T A K I T H L H A N Y E E O C A
T G B R H O S E M U V T U Y R C T E
A W I P U S K H A K S H S T B K O S
E A L O B S T E R S A M Y Q O R P W
S O S A L T L K L E B A S H U E U A
D V E D A E V Y I J E L L Y F I S H
W H A L E J O O N E S C S A N D D K
```

EVERYTHING KIDS

ANSWERS

Let's Play

What's a shark's favorite game?

S W A L L O W
smack, yummy, gulp, urp, urp, slurp, yummy

T H E
yum, crunch, munch

L E A D E R
urp, munch, gulp, gurgle, munch, crack

Funny Fish

What are the most expensive
fish at the pet store?

G O L D F I S H
1. 2. 3. 4. 5. 6. 7. 8.

Under the Sea

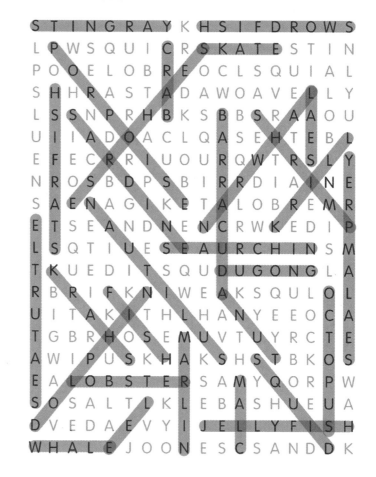

Blast Into Outer Space

How Many Moons?

Our moon is much smaller than the Earth. How much smaller? Complete the following equation to find out how many moons you would have to add together to equal one planet Earth.

_____ number of planets in our solar system

+_____ number of dwarf planets named "Pluto"

+_____ number of hours for one Earth rotation

+_____ number of full moons in a year

x_____ number of years in 24 months

-_____ number of letters in "moon phases"

=_____ number of moons to make one Earth

Confusing Comets

This astronomer is searching for a special comet, but there seem to be a lot of choices! Which is the one he wants? Use the clues to find out!

The correct comet...

...must have 4 tails

...must have the tails on the left side

...must be round

...must be smooth

Long Journey

Neptune is located at the outer edge of our solar system, so it takes a long time to travel all the way around the sun. In fact, even though Neptune was discovered in 1846, it still has not made one complete orbit since! Use the following rules to cross numbers out of the grid. The remaining number will tell you how many Earth-years equal one Neptune-year!

Cross out numbers...

...with two zeroes

...with three digits that add up to 8

...that are divisible by 2

200	620	222	1010
2030	305	422	611
910	500	161	125
341	2007	165	442
142	820	710	300

YOU ARE HERE

8. _____

7. _____

6. _____

5. _____

4. _____

3. _____

2. _____

1. _____

SOLAR SYSTEM · NORTHERN HEMISPHERE · MILKY WAY GALAXY · ORION ARM · NORTH AMERICA · PLANET EARTH · UNIVERSE · YOUR STATE

It is always good to know your place in the universe! Can you put the place names that are scattered around the page in order from small to large?

— Write the name of the smallest place on line 1.

— Write the next bigger place on line 2.

— Keep going until you reach the biggest place on line 8!

HINT: Each swirling part of the Milky Way Galaxy is called an "arm."

FUN FACT

Sun or Star?

Any star the same size of Earth's sun or smaller is considered to be a dwarf star. The sun is known as a yellow dwarf star.

ANSWERS

How Many Moons?

  <u>8</u> number of planets in our solar system

+ <u>1</u> number of dwarf planets named "Pluto"

+ <u>24</u> number of hours for one Earth rotation

+ <u>12</u> number of full moons in a year

x <u>2</u> number of years in 24 months

- <u>10</u> number of letters in "moon phases"

= <u>80</u> number of moons to make one Earth

Long Journey

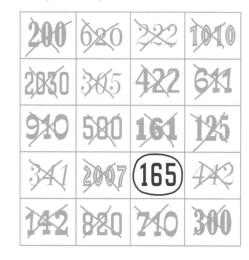

200	620	222	1010
2030	305	422	611
910	580	161	125
341	2007	(165)	442
142	820	710	300

Confusing Comets

You Are Here

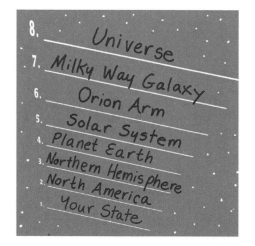

8. Universe
7. Milky Way Galaxy
6. Orion Arm
5. Solar System
4. Planet Earth
3. Northern Hemisphere
2. North America
1. Your State

COOL CARS

Fast Cars

There are at least 10 differences in these two collections of fast cars. How many can you find?

Zzzzzzzz

Break the Nutz 'n' Boltz Code to find the silly answer to this riddle:

Why don't racecars use mufflers?

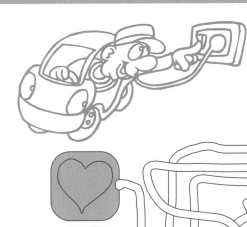

Electric Cars

Some car engines run on electricity, not gasoline. Can you untangle the crazy mess of electrical wires below? Draw a symbol in each empty box so that the wires connect to identical symbols.

Bye Bye

A "top fuel" car, or drag racer, can travel over 600 feet in less than three seconds. To do this, it reaches speeds of more than 270 miles per hour! This kind of super performance is tough on tires. How long do you think one of these high-tech tires will last? To find out, start at the letter marked with a white dot. Move clockwise around the circle picking up every third letter. Write them on the lines below.

A tire on a top fuel racecar lasts about

T H _ _ _ _ _   _ _ _ _ _ _ _ _ !

EVERYTHING KIDS

ANSWERS

Fast Cars

Electric Cars

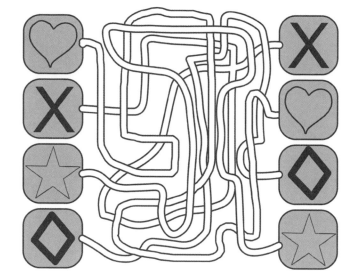

Zzzzzzzz

IT MAKES
THEM
EXHAUSTED

Bye Bye

THIRTY SECONDS!

Lunchtime Laughs

Eat Right

Find the names of the good-for-you foods listed in the food pyramid.

VEGETABLES
FRUITS
BEANS
MEAT
MILK
OILS
GRAINS

```
            P
        O   V   M
        S   E   M
        I A G I E
      B T R E R H T
      L D F T A A E
    K E S R A M T I I
  N O N E U B H O P N L
  Y A I M I L K W H I S
  E E E H L T E R U O Y L E
A B A R T I S S S S T L L I B
```

Extra fun: This medical expert specializes in knowing which foods keep you strong and healthy. Break the code to learn the name of this person's very important job.

A+3	H+1	H-3	S+1	G+2	V-2	F+3	C-2	L+2

What's going on here?

Cup   Plate
Fork   Knife
Spoon   Napkin
Glass   Saucer

Good Home Cookin'

Start at the letter marked with a dot. As you spiral into the center of the shell, collect every other letter. Write them in order on the lines below. When you reach the middle, head back out again, collecting all the letters that you skipped over the first time. Write these letters in order on the lines. When you are finished, you will have the answer to this riddle:

Where does a snail like to eat lunch?

```
    S   A A   N N
  R O S         F T
R E D R     T
L     O   O R   I.
  L U O A W
```

— — _ — — — — — — — — — — — — — !

Super Sandwich

This whopper of a sandwich contains 8 common ingredients between the slices of bread. How quickly can you find them?

Extra fun: Can you find the 2 hidden side orders that are often served with a sandwich?

CHEESE
HAM
LETTUCE
MAYONNAISE
MUSTARD
PICKLE
TOMATO
TURKEY

SIDE ORDERS:
_____
_____

```
M A Y O N N A I S E S A
P A I C W A L S E L O C
T U H K L S E L K C I P

M A Y M U S T A R D N P
O E S E E H C S T I W Y
T O M A T O A T O T U R

H T U R K E Y T O I W S
A S P I H C O T A T O P
S N I H C L E T T U C E
```

What did the potato call his son?

Chip.

EVERYTHING KIDS

ANSWERS

Eat Right

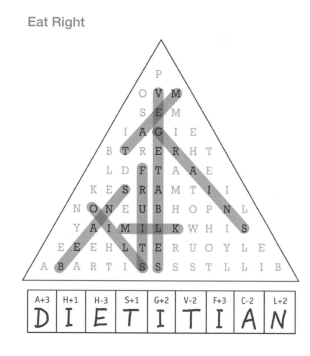

A+3	H+1	H-3	S+1	G+2	V-2	F+3	C-2	L+2
D	I	E	T	I	T	I	A	N

What's going on here?

The second word in each pair begins with the same letter as the last letter of the first word

Super Sandwich

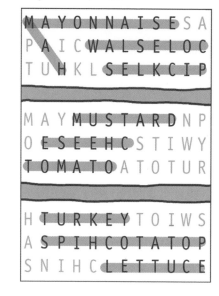

The 2 hidden side orders are COLESLAW and POTATO CHIPS.

Good Home Cookin'

Where does a snail like to eat lunch?

IN A SLOW FOOD RESTAURANT!

Shiver Me Timbers!

Yuck!

Since pirates couldn't stop at the market regularly, their food was often foul, rotten, or full of bugs. Sometimes there was no food at all! Then what did pirates eat? Read the numbered words to find an actual recipe for "Starvation Stew."

30 water	23 smaller	8 soak.
11 stones	5 thin	28 lots
7 and	14 tender.	18 hair,
22 into	20 roast.	1 Slice
16 off	2 leather	17 the
13 make	24 pieces	9 Beat
4 into	3 knapsack	12 to
27 with	6 pieces	19 then
15 Scrape	26 serve	25 and
10 between	21 Cut	29 of

Yum!

When food was plentiful, pirates dined on a special stew made from an unusual combination of foods. Unscramble each of the ingredients, then read the shaded letters from top to bottom to find the name of this pirate "delicacy." Would you eat a bowl full of this?

SHIF = _ _ _ _

BRAC = _ _ _ _

RAGCLI = _ _ _ _ _ _

TEAM = _ _ _ _

GABBACE = _ _ _ _ _ _ _

GRINEVA = _ _ _ _ _ _ _

TRUIF = _ _ _ _ _

OONIN = _ _ _ _ _

RAHD-LOIBED SEGG = _ _ _ _-_ _ _ _ _ _ _ _ _ _

SCIPES = _ _ _ _ _ _

Scrub-a-Dub-Dub

Help the pirate scrub his ship from STERN (very back) to PROW (very front).

PROW

STERN

Sing as You Work

Sea shanties were work songs sung by the pirates. These songs or chants had strong, simple rhythms that helped the pirates keep in time with each other. Shanties were sung especially when doing hard work, such as lifting the enormous anchor! Using the key provided, decode the lyrics to this shanty popular during the age of the great sailing ships.

T		MY	W	-		,	AH!
WE'			PAY	PA		Y	YLE
F	R	H	S	B		TS.
T		MY	W			,	AH!
WE'		A		THR	W		T
AT	THE	C		K.
T		MY	W		-		,	AH!
WE'		A				NK
B	AN	Y	AN	G	N.

Hint: Put the answer letters right over the symbols in the shanty.

AY	(cutlass)	O	(eye)
LL	(bone)	D	(hourglass)
I	(cannon)	R	(skull)

Silly Sentences

What is happening onboard this pirate ship today? Figure out what letter can finish all the words in each sentence to find out!

__razy __ooks __hop __arrots.

__ails __lap __even __illy __eagulls.

__ild __ind __hips __et __hitecaps.

__irates __ractice __lundering.

__ats __ehearse __igging __aces.

__rightening __lags __lap __itfully.

EVERYTHING KIDS

ANSWERS

Yuck!

Slice leather knapsack into thin pieces and soak. Beat between stones to make tender. Scrape off the hair, then roast. Cut into smaller pieces and serve with lots of water.

Silly Sentences

<u>C</u>razy <u>C</u>ooks <u>C</u>hop <u>C</u>arrots.
<u>S</u>ails <u>S</u>lap <u>S</u>even <u>S</u>illy <u>S</u>eagulls.
<u>W</u>ild <u>W</u>ind <u>W</u>hips <u>W</u>et <u>W</u>hitecaps.
<u>P</u>irates <u>P</u>ractice <u>P</u>lundering.
<u>R</u>ats <u>R</u>ehearse <u>R</u>igging <u>R</u>aces.
<u>F</u>rightening <u>F</u>lags <u>F</u>lap <u>F</u>itfully.

Yum!

SHIF = <u>F</u>I<u>S</u>H
BRAC = <u>C</u>R<u>A</u>B
RAGCLI = <u>GA</u>R<u>LI</u>C
TEAM = <u>M</u>E<u>A</u>T
GABBACE = <u>CABBA</u>GE
GRINEVA = <u>VINE</u>G<u>AR</u>
TRUIF = <u>FRUI</u>T
OONIN = <u>ONIO</u>N
RAHD-LOIBED SEGG = <u>HARD</u>-<u>BOILED</u> <u>EGGS</u>
SCIPES = <u>S</u>P<u>I</u>CE<u>S</u>

Pirate stew is "SALMAGUNDI"

Scrub-a-Dub-Dub

Sing as You Work

Ready to Recycle?

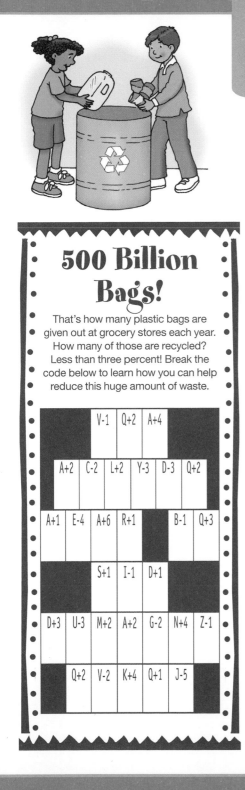

500 Billion Bags!

That's how many plastic bags are given out at grocery stores each year. How many of those are recycled? Less than three percent! Break the code below to learn how you can help reduce this huge amount of waste.

	V-1	Q+2	A+4		
A+2	C-2	L+2	Y-3	D-3	Q+2
A+1	E-4	A+6	R+1		B-1	Q+3
		S+1	I-1	D+1		
D+3	U-3	M+2	A+2	G-2	N+4	Z-1
	Q+2	V-2	K+4	Q+1	J-5	

Much Too Much!

Use the decoder to figure out how one student took recycling a little too far!

Teacher: Where is your homework?

Student: _ m _ d _ _ t _ n t
_ p _ p _ r _ _ r p l _ n _
_ n d _ t g _ t h _ j _ c k _ d !

A E I O

Jar Art

Some materials can be recycled without ever leaving the house! What could you do with these empty jars? Break the Vowel-Switch code to find out. Then use your markers or crayons to complete the transformation!

COTCH LAGHTNANG BIGS

VOSU FER WALD FLEWURS

STERU LUFTEVURS AN FRADGU

CELLUCT ELD BITTENS

Reuse That Junk

See how many useful items you can spell by using the letters in

N-E-W-S-P-A-P-E-R-S
and J-U-N-K M-A-I-L.

1. _____
2. _____
3. _____
4. _____
5. _____
6. _____
7. _____
8. _____
9. _____
10. _____
11. _____
12. _____
13. _____
14. _____
15. _____

EVERYTHING KIDS

ANSWERS

500 Billion Bags!

V-1 **U**	Q+2 **S**	A+4 **E**
A+2 **C**	C-2 **A**	L+2 **N**	Y-3 **V**	D-3 **A**	Q+2 **S**
A+1 **B**	E-4 **A**	A+6 **G**	R+1 **S**		B-1 **A**	Q+3 **T**
	S+1 **T**	I-1 **H**	D+1 **E**		
D+3 **G**	U-3 **R**	M+2 **O**	A+2 **C**	G-2 **E**	N+4 **R**	Z-1 **Y**
	Q+2 **S**	V-2 **T**	K+4 **O**	Q+1 **R**	J-5 **E**

USE CANVAS BAGS AT THE GROCERY STORE

Much Too Much!

Teacher: Where is your homework?

Student: I made it into
a paper airplane
and it got hijacked!

Jar Art

CATCH LIGHTNING BUGS

VASE FOR WILD FLOWERS

STORE LEFTOVERS IN FRIDGE

COLLECT OLD BUTTONS

Reuse That Junk

Everyone will have different words — here are some examples:

SAIL	**PAN**
NAIL	**PIN**
PAIL	**SINK**
JAR	**SAW**
PEN	**INK**
PLANE	**SKIS**
PLANK	**WIPES**
JEWELS	**JEANS**
PUMP	

Rainforest Animals

Biiiiiig Snake

The biggest snake ever found was 28 feet long, and 44 inches around the middle. Scientists estimate that this snake weighed over 500 pounds! What is this giant's name? Place a letter in each space to make a three-letter word from left to right (we gave you a few hints). When you have done it correctly, you will find the answer spelled for you in the shaded boxes.

made of tin	C	A	N
before two	O	N	E
girl's nickname	P	A	T
frozen water	I	C	E
cat chaser	D	O	G
picnic insect	A	N	T
not even	O	D	D
lunch sack	B	A	G

Extra Fun:
If a minivan is 16 feet long, how many minivans long is this snake?

Breezy Butterflies

Believe it or not, there isn't much wind in a rainforest! Most rainforest plants need the animals and insects who live there to move their pollen and seeds around. Butterflies flit from flower to flower drinking nectar, and carry pollen from one plant to another as they go.

Draw the second half of this butterfly to match the half shown. Use the grid lines to guide you.

ART AUG

Who Am I?

Find the capital letter in each clue below that does not start the sentence. Unscramble the six letters to find the name of this mysterious rainforest cat.

I am the largest cat in the Americas.

I am a solitaRy animal.

I have powerful Jaws.

I swim And climb very well.

I like to ambUsh my prey.

I snarl and Growl.

JAGUAR

Slow as a Sloth

The sloth doesn't do anything fast. He moves so slowly that a kind of plant called algae grows on him! In the grid below are three words that also mean slow. To find them, take one letter from each column moving left to right. **HINT:** Each letter can only be used once, so cross them off as you go.

```
L   D   K   E
I   O   Z   Y
P   A   L   Y
P   A   L   Y
```

1. _____
2. _____
3. _____

In Hiding

Sloths have such thick fur that they are the perfect camping place for smaller rainforest creatures. Scientists found one sloth that had three kinds of beetles, and three kinds of moths living on it! Can you find the 12 other things hiding in this sloth's fur? Look for an umbrella, candle, jumprope, paper clip, comb, feather, bowling pin, Christmas tree, fish hook, capital letter M, spatula, pencil.

EVERYTHING KIDS

ANSWERS

Biiiiiig Snake

clue			
made of tin	C	A	N
before two	O	N	E
girl's nickname	P	A	T
frozen water	I	C	E
cat chaser	D	O	G
picnic insect	A	N	T
not even	O	D	D
lunch sack	B	A	G

Extra Fun

The snake is as long as 1¾ minivans (28 ÷ 16 = 1¾).

Breezy Butterflies

Who Am I?

JAGUAR

Slow as a Sloth

1. LAZY
2. IDLE
3. POKY

In Hiding

Jurassic Jungle

If at first . . .

Cross out each letter below that appears more than five times. Collect the remaining letters from left to right and top to bottom, and write them in the spaces. When you're finished, you'll have the answer to this riddle:

What do you call a dinosaur that never gives up?

T B R N B Y
B T R B Y N
T N R Y N C
E B R B A N
T O N P B S

_ _ _ _ _ _ _

_ _ _ _ _

I can do it!

What is an Iguanodon's favorite playground toy?

A dino-see-saur!

Heads or Tails

Place each of the words into the boxes in alphabetical order, starting across the top row and working your way down to the bottom row. When you're finished, read down the shaded column to answer to this riddle:

What does a Triceratops sit on? Its . . .

GUM
DEBIT
CRY
ART
GONE
FEAT
BUCK
BITE
DATE
FATE
ACT
DOG
BYE

Prehistoric Pairs

Can you find the pair of Triceratops skulls that match exactly?

What is noisier than a Hadrosaurus?

Color in the shapes that contain the letters N-O-I-S-E and you will find out!

EVERYTHING KIDS

ANSWERS

If at first . . .

T̶B̶R̶A̶B̶Y
B̶T̶R̶B̶Y̶N̶
T̶N̶R̶Y̶N̶C
E̶B̶R̶B̶A̶N̶
T̶O̶M̶P̶B̶S

<u>TRY-TRY-TRY-</u>
<u>CERATOPS</u>

Heads or Tails

A	C	**T**		
A	**R**	T		
B	I	**T**	E	
B	U	**C**	K	
B	Y			
C	**R**	Y		
D	**A**	T	E	
D	E	**B**	I	T
D	**O**	G		
F	A	**T**	E	
F	E	A	**T**	
G	**O**	N	E	
G	U	**M**		

Prehistoric Pairs

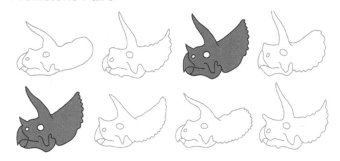

What is noisier than a Hadrosaurus?

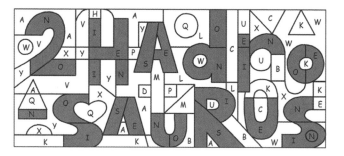

CLOUDY with a chance of FUN!

What nickname do weather forecasters call their baby boys?

Use a simple number substitution code (A=1, B=2, C=3 . . .) to find out!

Where's the Weather?

There are 13 weather words hiding in these sentences. Can you find them all?

How independent Kevin is now!

I certainly hope the river runs under our house.

Kami stole the cobra in Concord.

The twins were both under the bed.

Two gruff ogres hum identical tunes.

The Earth ails when recycling fails.

Winston scolds Eric loudly.

The aisle Ethan walked down was skinny.

WORD LIST

fog	humid
cold	hail
ice	cloud
sun	sleet
mist	thunder
rain	wind
snow	

Zany Rainy

Ramona and Celeste are twins who do everything together, even jumping in puddles! Can you find the 10 differences between the pictures of the girls enjoying a rainy day?

Rain Man, Sun Man

No one wants poor Rain Man at the beach! Can you help him move through the maze until he turns into a sunny day? Make a path that alternates between rain and sun. You can move up and down, or side-to-side, but not diagonally. If you hit a cloudy day, you are going the wrong way!

START
END

What Is a Tree's Favorite Drink?

Fill in all shapes marked with the letters G-U-L-P to find out!

Hide-and-Seek

Put the animal names scattered on this puzzle into the proper blanks to form new words. **HINT:** Some names can be used more than once, and one won't be used at all!

BEAR   FLY   PIG   BIRD   COW   ANT   DOG   CAT   LION

1. _ _ _ WOOD
2. S _ _ _ L
3. MIL _ _ _ _
4. _ _ _ EON
5. S _ _ _ TER
6. _ _ _ _ HOUSE
7. _ _ _ BOY
8. STIF _ _ _
9. S _ _ _ OT
10. _ _ _ _ DS

EVERYTHING KIDS

ANSWERS

Zany Rainy

What nickname do . . .

Rain Man, Sun Man

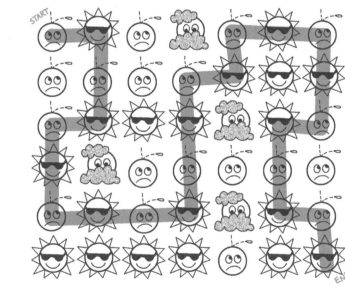

Where's the Weather?

How independent Kevin is now!

I certainly hope the river runs under our house.

Kami stole the cobra in Concord.

The twins were both under the bed.

Two gruff ogres hum identical tunes.

The Earth ails when recycling fails.

Winston scolds Eric loudly.

The aisle Ethan walked down was skinny.

What Is a Tree's Favorite Drink?

Hide-and-Seek

1. D O G WOOD
2. S C O W L
3. MIL L I O N
4. P I G EON
5. S C A T TER
6. B I R D HOUSE
7. C O W BOY
8. STIF F L Y
9. S P I G OT
10. B E A R DS

Storybook Princesses

One Hundred Years

Sleeping Beauty slept for one hundred years. Find all of the columns and rows in this castle wall where the numbers add up to exactly one hundred. One of the answers has already been found

25	18	16	10	21	7	18
7	20	23	10	9	24	4
8	27	7	0	15	12	12
25	3	4	22	24	5	17
16	5	12	18	11	9	22
7	4	27	10	9	20	23
12	10	15	0	11	24	5

Save the Prince

Which rope should the mermaid pull to save the Prince?

The Secret Answer

The Queen asked, "Mirror, mirror on the wall, who is the fairest one of all?" Knowing the answer would anger the queen, the mirror displayed the answer in code. Can you figure out the answer? A substitution code is used where 1=A, 2=B, and so on.

$\overline{19\ 14\ 15\ 23}$ $\overline{23\ 8\ 9\ 20\ 5}$

$\overline{9\ 19}$ $\overline{1}$

$\overline{20\ 8\ 15\ 21\ 19\ 1\ 14\ 4}$

$\overline{20\ 9\ 13\ 5\ 19}$ $\overline{6\ 1\ 9\ 18\ 5\ 18}$

$\overline{20\ 8\ 1\ 14}$ $\overline{25\ 15\ 21}$!

Kissing Frogs

You have to kiss a lot of frogs to find a prince! Can you find the frog that will turn into a prince? It is the one that is in an oval and a triangle, but not in a rectangle.

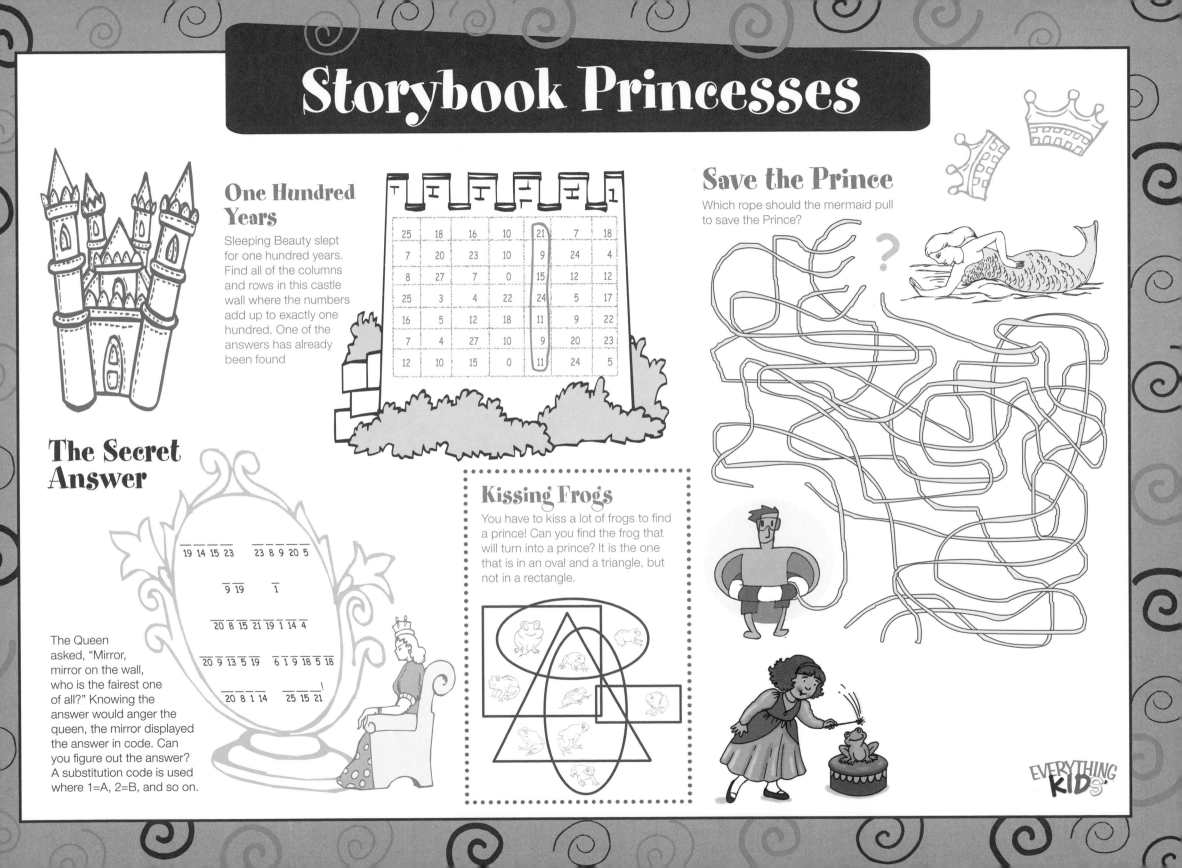

ANSWERS

One Hundred Years

25	18	16	10	21	7	18
7	20	23	10	9	24	4
8	27	7	0	15	12	12
25	3	4	22	24	5	17
16	5	12	18	11	9	22
7	4	27	10	9	20	23
12	10	15	0	11	24	5

Save the Prince

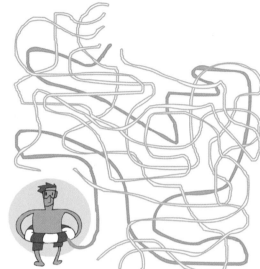

The Secret Answer

SNOW   WHITE
IS   A
THOUSAND
TIMES   FAIRER
THAN   YOU!

Kissing Frogs

Grassland Animals

You Snooze, You Lose

If you move slowly in the grasslands, you will probably be caught by a predator. Can you help these antelope find the correct path through this grid using only "fast" words? You can move up and down and side to side, but not diagonally.

START

RUN	STOP	DOZE	SMILE	SWIFT
SPRINT	SPEED	SLEEP	GO	STOP
STAND	HURRY	RACE	LAZY	STROLL
DAWDLE	PAUSE	SCURRY	GALLOP	HUSTLE

END

Hide and Eat

Grasslands feed many herds of plant-eating animals (herbivores). These herds attract the meat-eating animals (carnivores) that hunt them. Look carefully to find and highlight all the herbivores and carnivores hidden in the grass.

Try using different colored markers to highlight each type—how about green for herbivores and red for carnivores?

```
G R A S S G R A S S G R A S S
R O P P I H G R A L I O N G G
A G R A S C G R A S R S G B R
S N B G R H A S S G A R A U A
S I I G Z E B R A R F A R Z S
G D S R A E G R A S F S O Z S
R W O L F T R A E S E G S A G
A G N R G A A S L G A R T R R
S R A H R H S L E O P A R D A
S A S Y A G S G P A R S I S S
G A Z E L L E R H G R A C S S
R S G N S G R A A S S R H G G
A G R A S A S G N R A S S R R
S G R A S V U L T U R E A A A
S M E R V I N G R A S S G R S
G R A S S G R A S S G R A S S
```

Herbivores:
Zebra
Gazelle
Giraffe
Bison
Hippo
Elephant
Ostrich
Mervin

Carnivores:
Cheetah
Hyena
Lion
Vulture
Buzzard
Leopard
Dingo
Wolf

Marvelous Meadowlark

The meadowlark is one of the most common birds of the American grasslands. More than 121,000 Kansas schoolchildren voted to award this beautiful black and yellow bird a special honor. Collect the letters hidden in each section of this field. Unscramble them to see what award the meadowlark won.

K S A A T E R B
K N A S S A T A E R D I
N S T A S

Poor Rhino

High prices are paid for the horns of rhinoceroses. Why would anyone want them? To find out, answer each question below and put the letters into their proper place in the grid. Work back and forth until you have the answer.

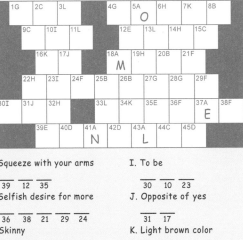

1G	2C	3L		4G	5A	6H	7K	8B
9C	10I	11L		12E	13L	14H	15C	
	16K	17J		18A M	19H	20B	21F	
22H	23I	24F	25B	26B	27G	28G	29F	
30I	31J	32H		33L	34K	35E	36F	37A E	38F
	39E	40D	41A N	42D	43A L	44C	45D	

A. Sour fruit
L E M O N
43 37 18 5 41

B. To be ill
_ _ _ _
8 25 26 20

C. Body part under a hat
_ _ _ _
2 44 9 15

D. Unhappy
_ _ _
45 40 42

E. Squeeze with your arms
_ _ _
39 12 35

F. Selfish desire for more
_ _ _ _ _
36 38 21 29 24

G. Skinny
_ _ _ _
1 4 27 28

H. Picture in your sleep
_ _ _ _ _
32 6 14 19 22

I. To be
_ _ _
30 10 23

J. Opposite of yes
_ _
31 17

K. Light brown color
_ _ _
16 34 7

L. What a plant grows from
_ _ _ _
13 3 11 33

The Watering Hole

Look at these six pictures. Number them in order so that the story makes sense.

EVERYTHING KIDS

ANSWERS

You Snooze, You Lose

START

RUN	*STOP*	*DOZE*	*SMILE*	*SWIFT*
SPRINT	*SPEED*	*SLEEP*	*GO*	*SCURRY*
STAND	*HURRY*	*SCURRY*	*LAZY*	*STOP*
DAWDLE	*PAUSE*	*SPRINT*	*GALLOP*	*HUSTLE*

END

Marvelous Meadowlark

KANSAS STATE BIRD

K S A A T A E R B
N A S T T A S D I

Hide and Eat

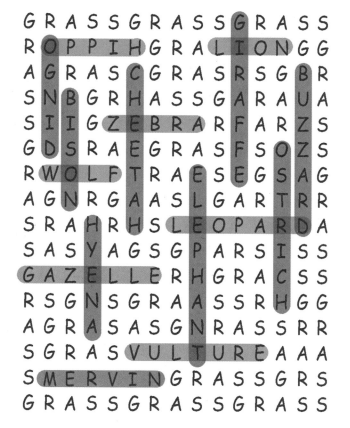

G R A S S G R A S S G R A S S
R O P P I H G R A L I O N G G
A G R A S C G R A S R S G B R
S N B G R H A S S G A R A U A
S I I G Z E B R A R F A R Z S
G D S R A E G R A S F S O Z S
R W O L F T R A E S E G S A G
A G N R G A A S L G A R T R R
S R A H R H S L E O P A R D A
S A S Y A G S G P A R S I S S
G A Z E L L E R H G R A C S S
R S G N S G R A A S S R H G G
A G R A S A S G N R A S S R R
S G R A S V U L T U R E A A A
S M E R V I N G R A S S G R S
G R A S S G R A S S G R A S S

Poor Rhino

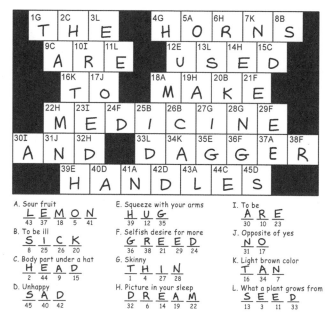

1G T	2C H	3L E		4G H	5A O	6H R	7K N	8B S
9C A	10I R	11L E		12E U	13L S	14H E	15C D	
16K T	17J O		18A M	19H A	20B K	21F E		
22H M	23I E	24F D	25B I	26B C	27G I	28G N	29F E	
30I A	31J N	32H D		33L D	34K A	35E G	36F G	37A E	38F R
	39E H	40D A	41A N	42D D	43A L	44C E	45D S	

A. Sour fruit
L E M O N
43 37 18 5 41

E. Squeeze with your arms
H U G
39 12 35

I. To be
A R E
30 10 23

B. To be ill
S I C K
8 25 26 20

F. Selfish desire for more
G R E E D
36 38 21 29 24

J. Opposite of yes
N O
31 17

C. Body part under a hat
H E A D
2 44 9 15

G. Skinny
T H I N
1 4 27 28

K. Light brown color
T A N
16 34 7

D. Unhappy
S A D
45 40 42

H. Picture in your sleep
D R E A M
32 6 14 19 22

L. What a plant grows from
S E E D
13 3 11 33

The Watering Hole

I Scream, You Scream

Ice Cream Trivia

What is the most popular ice cream topping?

What is the most popular ice cream flavor?

Who was the first U.S. President to eat ice cream?

The first hand-cranked ice cream freezer was patented in what year: 1848, 1904, or 1955?

Favorite Flavors

Find all of the flavors in this ice cream cone by looking up, down, across, backward, and diagonally. Some letters may appear in more than one word.

```
                    H D I
               T U N O C O C O B
          R D F T F J V T A T G I G
         M J F K U V O T N R O E F A C W Q
        L E M O N H T P I S T A C H I O A B P
       N W V O L F C O M V L G I S S C F L I M E
      Y R R E B W A R T S E K H H P R F N B O Q
     G N A Z B L U E B E R R Y R Q E B E U L B B K
      K D A Y D J P P R F V A N I L L A E T I Z B S
     Q N H C C I P C P N T O K B K Z P N H R T O Z T L
     A S I J A E T A L O C O H C A P T A B T R U G J R
     P D U H P G P H D A J M X Q L O M N I D D Y B W J
     L X W O T Z K W I K R G C H E R R Y A A S B X D J A Y
```

VANILLA
CHOCOLATE
STRAWBERRY
BANANA
PEACH
COFFEE
RASPBERRY
CHERRY
LEMON
BLUEBERRY
PINEAPPLE

COCONUT
PISTACHIO
HAZELNUT
MINT
PEPPERMINT
LIME
BUTTERSCOTCH
PECAN
WALNUT

The Next Ice Cream Bar

Can you guess which ice cream bar will be given after the first two?

1. OR
2. OR
3. OR
4. OR
5. OR

Sharing

Olivia, Louis, and Paul want to buy a 30-cent ice cream bar to share. If they put all of their money together, will it be enough? How much money does each person have?

Olivia and Louis together have a total of 18 cents.
Louis and Paul together have a total of 23 cents.
Paul and Olivia together have a total of 19 cents.

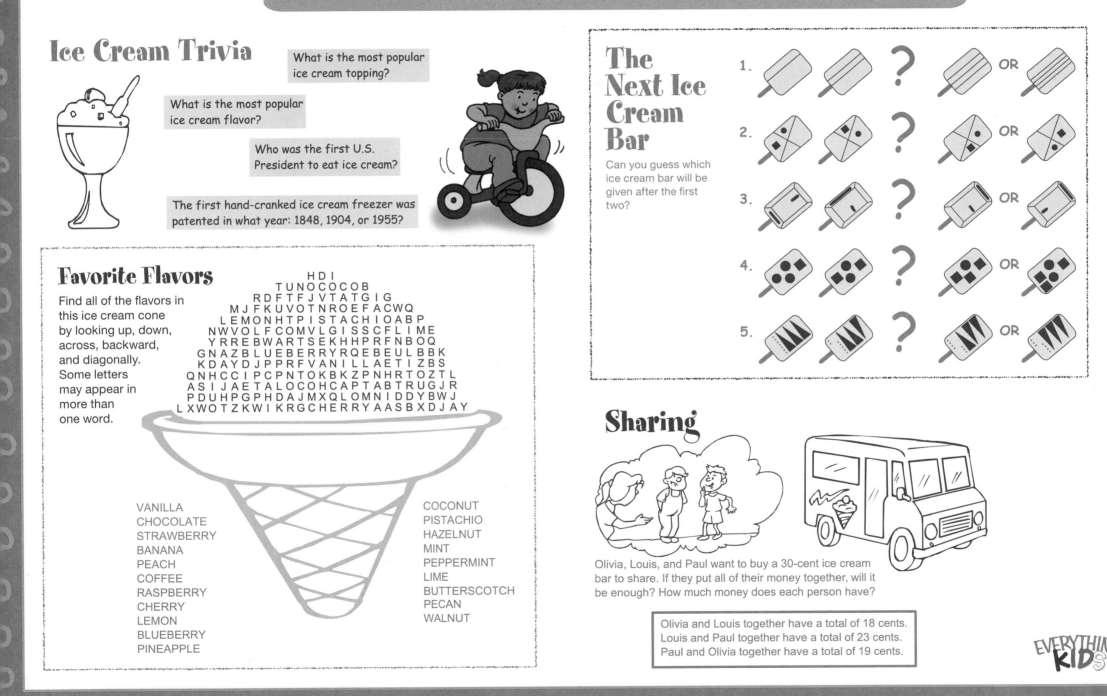

ANSWERS

Ice Cream Trivia

Chocolate syrup is the most popular topping for ice cream.

Vanilla is by far the most popular flavor of ice cream.

George Washington was the first U.S. President to eat ice cream. He loved ice cream!

The first hand-cranked ice cream freezer was patented in the year **1848**.

Favorite Flavors

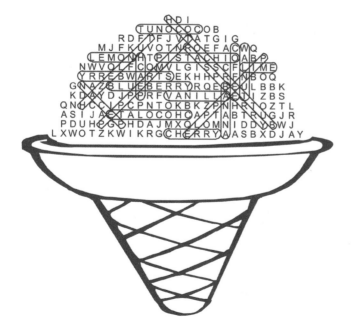

The Next Ice Cream Bar

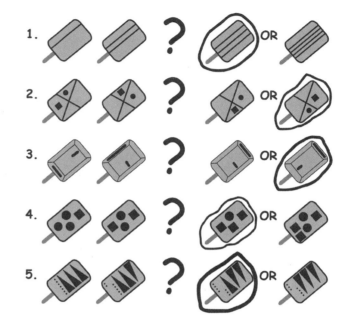

Sharing

Olivia has 7 cents.
Louis has 11 cents.
Paul has 12 cents.
Together they have 30 cents, just enough to buy the ice cream bar.

PARTY TIME!

Cake-o-licious

Everyone has their favorite kind of cake. What sort of cake do you think each of these characters likes best? When you have decided, see if you can fit the cake names into the puzzle grid. We left you a B-I-T-E of I-C-I-N-G to get you started!

Hink Pinks

The answers to these riddles are two single-syllable words that rhyme. Can you figure out these party hink pinks?

A quick present = _ _ _ _ _ _   _ _ _ _

A not real dessert = _ _ _ _   _ _ _ _ _

A dumb party activity = _ _ _ _ _   _ _ _ _

Kooky Carnival

How many weird or wacky things can you find at this backyard carnival?

FOURTUNE TELER

PALM READING

KNOCK 'EM DOWN!

RING THE BELL

5¢

ICE COLD HOT DOGS

ROBERT for APPLES

Peculiari-tea

Tanika invited four friends to a tea party, but each guest wanted something different to drink! Break the code on each cup to see what kind of drinks Tanika made for her guests.

Milk

19-15-4-1

KVJDF

EVERYTHING KIDS

ANSWERS

Cake-o-licious

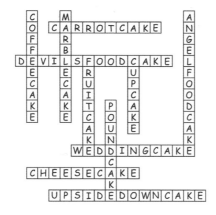

```
C   M               A
O  CARROTCAKE       N
F  A   R            G
F  R   B            E
DEVILSFOODCAKE      L
E  L   E   R   U    F
C  E   C   U   P    O
A  C   A   I   P    O
K  A   K   T   C    D
E  K   E   C   A    C
       FRUITCAKE    K
           P   K    E
          POUND     
           N   
       WEDDINGCAKE  
           D   
       CHEESECAKE
           A
           K
       UPSIDEDOWNCAKE
```

Peculiari-tea

MILK SHAKE

SODA
(Code: A=1, B=2, C=3, etc.)

JUICE
(Code: Substitute the letter before each letter of the message.)

ICED TEA

Hink Pinks

A quick present = S W I F T   G I F T

A not real dessert = F A K E   C A K E

A dumb party activity = L A M E   G A M E

Kooky Carnival

Almost everything at this carnival is kooky!

Start Your Engines!

Number One

One of the first auto races was held in 1887. But before the race ever started, it was cancelled! To find out why, cross out cars with letter pairs that have an I, F, or T. Read the remaining cars from left to right and top to bottom.

Fan Fun

Each sentence needs one letter to complete all the words. Have fun figuring out the silly things these race fans are doing!

__rantic __amilies __lap __estive __lags.

__razy __ouples __arry __ardboard __utouts.

__ild __omen __ave __acky __ooden __ands.

__ischievous __en __ake __onkey __oves.

__heering __hildren __ast __olorful __onfetti.

Rollover

Regain control of this car by moving one space at a time making compound words as you go. You can move up and down, and side to side, but not diagonally. If you succeed, your car will shortly be back in the road race!

START				
ROLL	OVER	SIDE	SHOW	TUNE
BACK	HAND	HILL	OFF	ROAD
STEP	MADE	UP	SCALE	WAY

END

Zap

At this first race, drivers wore suits and hats, the track was dirt, and most people in the crowd drove a horse and buggy. But there was one thing that seemed strangely modern: The winning car used a fuel that cars are just beginning to use today! Break the code to learn what it was.

W+2= ◯
V-2= ◯
H+1= ◯
B+1= ◯
K-2= ◯
Q+1= ◯
U-1= ◯
F-3= ◯
B+3= ◯
K+1= ◯
I-4= ◯

→ Oops, we forgot to say read this from bottom to top!

Fully Equipped

Stock cars are modeled after passenger cars, but because they are built for racing they have many special features. See if you can find all of these racecar parts hidden in this car. Use a highlight marker to run a single line of color through each word as you find it. When you are through, look at the crazy racing stripes this car will have!

kill switch
sway bar
firewall
TV camera
spoiler
smooth tires
big engines
no muffler
roll cage
fuel cell
data recorder

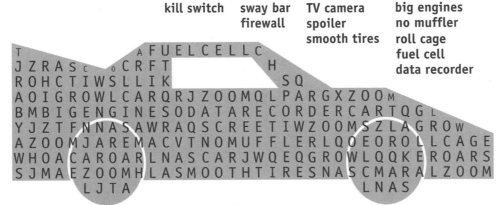

EVERYTHING KIDS

ANSWERS

Number One

Fan Fun

<u>F</u>rantic <u>F</u>amilies <u>F</u>lap <u>F</u>estive <u>F</u>lags.

<u>C</u>razy <u>C</u>ouples <u>C</u>arry <u>C</u>ardboard <u>C</u>utouts.

<u>W</u>ild <u>W</u>omen <u>W</u>ave <u>W</u>acky <u>W</u>ooden <u>W</u>ands.

<u>M</u>ischievous <u>M</u>en <u>M</u>ake <u>M</u>onkey <u>M</u>oves.

<u>C</u>heering <u>C</u>hildren <u>C</u>ast <u>C</u>olorful <u>C</u>onfetti.

Rollover

START				
ROLL	OVER	SIDE	SHOW	TUNE
BACK	HAND	HILL	OFF	ROAD
STEP	MADE	UP	SCALE	WAY END

Zap

W+2= Y
V-2= T
H+1= I
B+1= C
K-2= I
Q+1= R
U-1= T
F-3= C
B+3= E
K+1= L
I-4= E

Oops, we forgot to say read this from bottom to top!

Fully Equipped

Endangered Species

There's No Place Like Home

Mountain gorillas are gentle, giant apes that live in Central Africa. Unfortunately, much of their forest is being cleared for farmland. People who care about the gorillas are working hard to keep enough land as good gorilla habitat. You can help by crossing out all the harmful words in this grid. Circle the synonyms for PROTECT!

defend	neglect	destroy
secure	SUPPORT	care for
FAIL	guard	*ruin*	harm
ignore	burn	SHIELD
preserve	uproot	save
damage	shelter	rescue
watch over	HELP	*pollute*

Sad Panda/ Glad Panda

More and more people are trying to save endangered animals. You can help Sad Panda move through the maze so he is Happy Panda at the end! Make a path that alternates sad and glad. You can move up and down, or side-to-side, but not diagonally. If you hit a Mad Panda, you are going in the wrong direction!

What Can I Do?

Heather doesn't like to read about so many endangered animals. She decided to write a letter to her friend, Keith. Unfortunately, Heather's typing is not very good. Look at the keyboard, below. Can you figure out what went wrong—and what Heather was trying to say?

E3Q4   I385Y,

8 2970E   08I3   59

Y30*   QH8JQOW.

8   IH92   5YQ5

8W   6974   U9G.

*03QW3

5300   J3   J943!

Y3Q5Y34

```
1 2 3 4 5 6 7 8 9 * 
Tab  Q W E R T Y U I O P
Caps  A S D F G H J K L :
Shift  Z X C V B N M , . ?
Ctrl  Alt              Alt
```

Be Like Me!

Here is Keith's answer:

Dear Heather,
I protect the Earth's natural resources, including the animals. My job has a really long name. To find out what it is, crack the code and fill the correct letters into the boxes. Read the letters from top to bottom. You can be one too!

	= the third one
	= one before P
	= between M and O
	= two after Q
	= the fifth one
	= one before S
	= between U and W
	= the first one
	= one after S
	= between H and J
	= three before R
	= two after L
	= three after F
	= between R and T
	= two before V

ANSWERS

There's No Place Like Home

(defend) ~~neglect~~ ~~destroy~~
(secure) (SUPPORT) (care for)
~~FAIL~~ (guard) ~~ruin~~ ~~harm~~
~~ignore~~ ~~burn~~ (SHIELD)
(preserve) ~~uproot~~ (save)
~~damage~~ (shelter) (rescue)
(watch over) (HELP) ~~pollute~~

Sad Panda/Glad Panda

What Can I Do?

E3Q4   I385Y,
DEAR KEITH,

8   2970E 08I3   59
I   WOULD LIKE TO

Y30*   QH8JQOW.
HELP   ANIMALS.

8   IH92   5YQ5
I   KNOW   THAT

8W   6974   U9G.
IS   YOUR   JOB.

 *03QW3
  PLEASE

5300   J3   J943!
TELL   ME   MORE!

Y3Q5Y34
HEATHER

Be Like Me!

C	= the third one
O	= one before P
N	= between M and O
S	= two after Q
E	= the fifth one
R	= one before S
V	= between U and W
A	= the first one
T	= one after S
I	= between H and J
O	= three before R
N	= two after L
I	= three after F
S	= between R and T
T	= two before V

Man's (and kid's) Best Friend

Dog Talk

Figure out the secret dog language and you'll know the answer to this riddle.

How do you keep a dog from barking in the front yard?

PBARKUBARKTBARK
HBARKIBARKMBARK
IBARKNBARK
TBARKHBARKEBARK
BBARKABARKCBARKKBARK
YBARKABARKRBARKDBARK!

Here, Rover?

Here's a list of the top ten names that people choose for their pets. To see which one is the MOST popular, cross out the following:

1. Cross out all the names that start with S.
2. Cross out all the names that end with Y.
3. Cross out all the names with four letters.
4. Cross out the name with GG.

Buddy   Molly
Bailey   Sadie
Jake   Sam
Max   Maggie
Nicky   Coco

Hungry Herd

Who will be the first pet to get breakfast? See if you can figure it out from the clues provided.

Ramona eats after Rosie. • Rosie eats before Stormy, but after Neudge.
Harry and Rosie eat together. • Stormy always eats last.

Stormy   Rosie

Harry

Ramona

Neudge

The Dog Walker

Can you tell which leash goes to which pet?

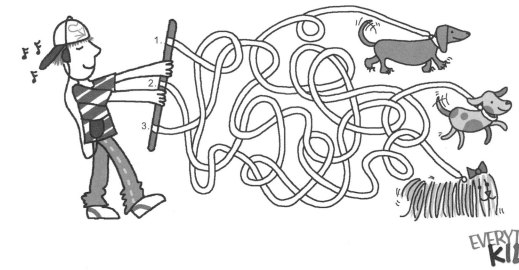

1.
2.
3.

EVERYTHING KIDS

ANSWERS

Dog Talk

The word BARK has been added after every letter in the answer! If you remove all the BARKs, the answer reads "Put him in the back yard!"

Here, Rover?

~~Buddy~~ ~~Molly~~

~~Bailey~~ ~~Sadie~~

~~Jake~~ ~~Sam~~

(Max) ~~Maggie~~

~~Nicky~~ ~~Coco~~

Hungry Herd

Neudge eats first.

The Dog Walker

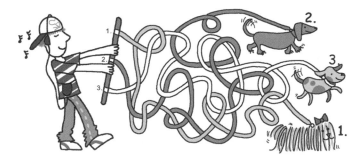

ROAD TRIP!

FUN FACT

History of the Car

The automobile was invented about 1890, but almost no one had a car until Henry Ford invented the Model T. Ford and his factory built the cars on an assembly line, a process that made everything faster. His company built 15 million Model T cars between 1908 and 1928.

To start early-model cars, you had to turn a crank, which made the spark that started the engine. Luckily for us, the cranks were eventually replaced with the modern car battery.

Fractured Bumper Stickers

Sort through these pieces from six bumper stickers and see if you can figure out their message.

1._____   4._____

2._____   5._____

3._____   6._____

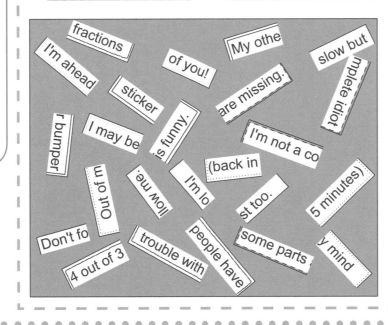

fractions
of you!
My othe
slow but
I'm ahead
sticker
are missing.
mplete idiot
r bumper
I may be
is funny.
I'm not a co
Out of m
llow me.
(back in
5 minutes)
I'm lo
st too.
Don't fo
people have
some parts
y mind
4 out of 3
trouble with

**Knock knock!
Who's there?
Honda.
Honda who?
Honda road again!**

What would you call a country where everyone drives a pink car?
Break this shifty code to find the answer:

B̄ Q̄J̄Ō L̄ D̄B̄S̄ Ō B̄Ū J̄P̄ Ō

Factoid: Use the same code to find out the most popular color for cars made in 2004: T̄ J̄ M̄ W̄ F̄ S̄

Mileage

Vince's car can travel 36 miles for every gallon of gas. Can you figure out which of these places Vince can visit if he has two and a half gallons of gas? The trip will start from home and return home. The numbers are the miles between points on the map.

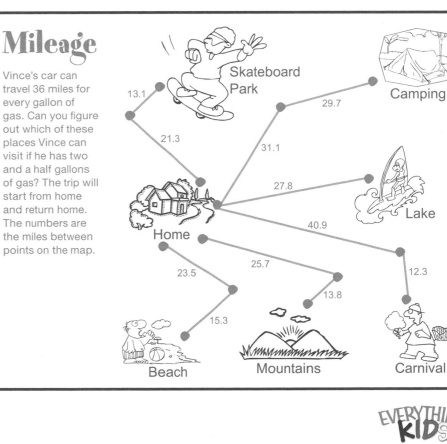

Skateboard Park
Camping
13.1
29.7
21.3
31.1
27.8
Lake
Home
40.9
23.5
25.7
12.3
15.3
13.8
Beach
Mountains
Carnival

EVERYTHING KIDS

ANSWERS

Fractured Bumper Stickers

1 Don't follow me.
I'm lost too.

2 I'm not a complete idiot
some parts are missing.

3 My other bumper
sticker is funny.

4 Out of my mind
(back in 5 minutes)

5 4 out of 3 people have
trouble with fractions

6 I may be slow but
I'm ahead of you!

What Would You Call . . .

A PINK CAR NATION

– ———— ——— ——————

B QJOL DBS OBUJPO

SILVER

——————

TJMWFS

Mileage

Vince can travel a total of 90 miles (2.5 gallons x 36 miles per gallon). This means that Vince can go up to 45 miles from home and still have enough gas to return. Adding up the mileage, we see that Vince can go to any of these places: **Skateboard Park**
Lake
Mountains
Beach

Delectable Dinnertime Delights

Dizzy Donuts

The Kruller family bought a baker's dozen donuts. Can you tell, by using the following clues, how many donuts each person ate? **HINT:** A baker's dozen = 13.

- **Dad ate twice as many donuts as Mom.**
- **Brooke ate fewer donuts than everyone else.**
- **Austin and Caleb ate the same number of donuts**

EXTRA FUN: Someone has taken a bite—and a letter—out of each of these donuts! Can you figure out what kinds of donuts were tasted?

Splash!

The ship's cook dropped dinner in the drink! Can you help him find his soggy supper? Look for a piece of cheese on a cracker, orange slice, apple, bowl of spaghetti, bowl of salad, slice of bread, stick of butter, glass of water, ice-cream cone, salt shaker, knife, fork, spoon, and teacup.

How Do You Make . . .

The new kid working at the snack bar is still learning his job. Look closely at the menu. Can you find the answer to his question?

How do you make a hotdog roll?

hoT dog   YOgurt   chiPs
Ice cream hambURger   grilLed cheese
miLk   sAlad
Tuna fish   Taco
                       french friEs

Put a different letter from the list into each empty box to make a familiar cooking word. The empty box might be at the beginning, the middle, or the end of the mystery word. **HINT:** Each letter in the list will be used only once.

When you are done, read down the shaded boxes to discover the answer to this curious cooking question:

Where should you go if you are a really, really bad cook?

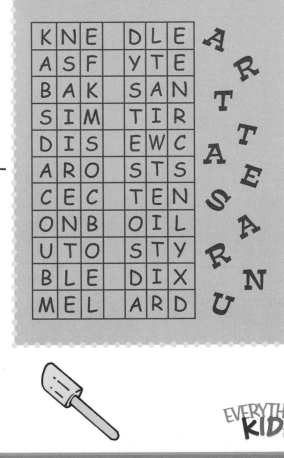

K	N	E		D	L	E
A	S	F		Y	T	E
B	A	K		S	A	N
S	I	M		T	I	R
D	I	S		E	W	C
A	R	O		S	T	S
C	E	C		T	E	N
O	N	B		O	I	L
U	T	O		S	T	Y
B	L	E		D	I	X
M	E	L		A	R	D

A R T T E A S R U N A T A S R U

EVERYTHING KIDS

ANSWERS

Dizzy Donuts

Chocolate
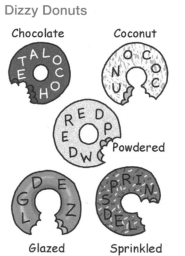

Coconut

Powdered

Glazed

Sprinkled

Dad ate 4 donuts, Mom ate 2, Austin ate 3, Caleb ate 3, and Brooke ate only 1 donut!

Splash!

Where should you go . . .

K	N	E	A	D	L	E
A	S	F	R	Y	T	E
B	A	K	E	S	A	N
S	I	M	S	T	I	R
D	I	S	T	E	W	C
A	R	O	A	S	T	S
C	E	C	U	T	E	N
O	N	B	R	O	I	L
U	T	O	A	S	T	Y
B	L	E	N	D	I	X
M	E	L	T	A	R	D

How Do You Make . . .

hoT dog   YOgurt   chiPs

Ice cream   hambURger   grilLed cheese

miLk   sAlad

Tuna fish   Taco

french friEs

Answer: Tilt your plate!

Seeing Stars

One in a Billion

With billions of stars in the sky, it's not easy to find one star in particular! Can you find the five-pointed star that is hiding in this corner of the galaxy?

Picture in the Sky

Use a white gel pen or white crayon to connect the numbers in order. The decoder will help you to spell out the name a Native American tribe used for this group of stars, long before it became known as the Big Dipper.

E☉ H★ K☆ N✶
S★ T✳ U★ Y✷

Found out in Space

ASTEROID   METEOR   PULSAR
BLACK HOLE MOON   RED GIANT
COMET   NEBULA   STAR
GALAXY   PLANET

Look carefully at this letter grid through your telescope. How many of the deep space objects from the word list can you find? Answers can go side to side, or up and down.

```
T W I P U L S A R N
K G L E T W I N E K
L A S T E R O I D E
L L I T T L E S G A
A A R P H O B W I L
W X O L N D L E A U
W Y H A A T A Y N B
U A R N E U C P T E
M E T E O R K B O N
O E T T H E H W O R
O L D S O C O M E T
N E B U H L L I K E
A S T A R D E I A M
```

Which One?

I can make things disappear and reappear simply by doing what I always do. Which one am I?

A. Eclipse

B. Supernova

C. Rocket

D. Comet

A. Eclipse

Twin Stars

Can you find the seven differences between this pair of twin stars?

EVERYTHING KIDS

ANSWERS

One in a Billion

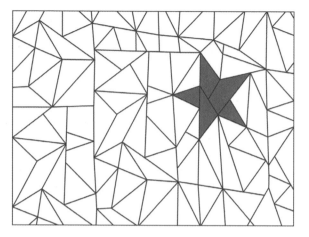

Picture in the Sky

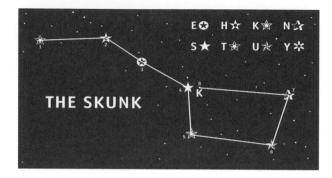

THE SKUNK

Found out in Space

Twin Stars

Seaworthy Sillies

Word to the Wise

Fish swim in schools because they feel safer that way. These words are trying to find the group they belong to. Write each word in the box where it belongs.*

hockey

robot

Chile

COUNTRY

ostrich

BIRD

soup

SPORTS

soccer

owl

golf

canoe

Greece

paddle

bread

robin

baseball

balloon

yacht

phone

Australia

apple

tofu

BOAT

FOOD

tomato

ferry

steamer

Finland

sparrow

football

radio

eagle

Japan

*Careful: There are 4 words that don't belong.

Dive at Your Own Risk!

It's too late now, but this diver has just noticed he's not going to be the only one in the pool. Can you see how many fish are already swimming around here?

Wet and Wild!

Even though most cats hate water, they love fish. It is believed that the ancestors of today's house cats lived in the marshes of Egypt, where they would have hunted all kinds of water animals, including frogs and birds.

Minnow Maze

This little minnow doesn't like being at the back of the school. Can you help him find his way to the front?

Watery Math

Just like you, this fish is going to school. Can you help him figure out which equations don't work?

$17 \times 3 = 51$

$15 + 16 + 17 + 18 = 50$

$48 - 37 = 11$

$135 \times 6 = 810$

$400 + 4 + 3 + 7 - 14 = 400$

$2 \times 200 + 34 = 434$

$11 - 7 + 678 = 683$

EVERYTHING KIDS

ANSWERS

Word to the Wise

SPORTS: hockey, golf, baseball, soccer, football
BIRD: ostrich, owl, robin, sparrow, eagle
COUNTRY: Chile, Greece, Japan, Australia, Finland
BOAT: canoe, yacht, paddle, steamer, ferry
FOOD: tofu, apple, soup, bread, tomato

Watery Math

$15 + 16 + 17 + 18 = 49$

$11 - 7 + 678 = 682$

Dive at Your Own Risk

There are 12 fish

Minnow Maze

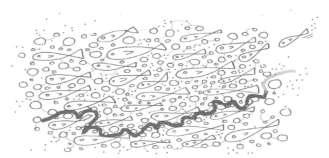

Dragon Tails

Boulder Dinner

How would you like stones for dinner? Dragons have such strong acid in their stomachs that they can digest boulders! Here's some other words with "ou" in them. Do you think dragons could eat these?

_ ou _ _

_ ou _ _ _ _ _

_ _ ou _

_ ou _ _ _

_ ou _ _ _ _ _

_ ou _

_ _ ou _

_ ou _ _

How do you make a dragon float? Two scoops of ice cream, soda water, a dragon, and a cherry on top!

Goo Goo

These twin baby dragons look exactly the same, but there are actually eleven differences. Can you spot them?

On a Scale of 1 to 10
You can tell the health of a dragon by looking at his scales. If he's feeling good they are bright and shiny. But if he's feeling ill they are dull and the color is grayish.

What time is it when you see a dragon in the kitchen making breakfast with your mom's dress on?

Time to wake up and go to school!

Happy Birthday, Dragon!

It's Jack the dragon's sixth birthday. It looks like a perfect sunny day, but can you find six things wrong with this picture?

HAPPY BIRTHDAY JOEY

WOOF!

ANSWERS

Boulder Dinner

HOUSE

MOUNTAIN

MOUNTIE

COUCH

FOUNTAIN

SCOUT

MOUSE

Goo Goo

Happy Birthday, Dragon!

1. "Birthday" is spelled wrong.

2. There are seven candles.

3. There are icicles in the summer.

4. His name is Jack, not Joey.

5. It's noon but the sun is setting.

6. The cat is barking.

Totally Turbo Trucks!

Scrambled Groceries

These trucks all deliver food to grocery stores. For some reason the letters on the trucks are scrambled. Can you figure out what each truck is delivring?

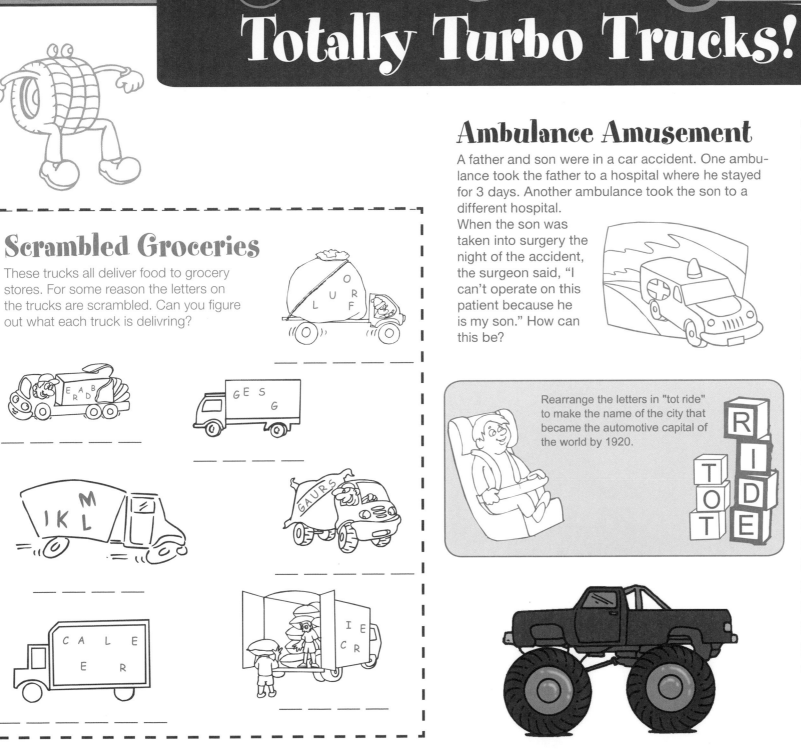

Ambulance Amusement

A father and son were in a car accident. One ambulance took the father to a hospital where he stayed for 3 days. Another ambulance took the son to a different hospital. When the son was taken into surgery the night of the accident, the surgeon said, "I can't operate on this patient because he is my son." How can this be?

Rearrange the letters in "tot ride" to make the name of the city that became the automotive capital of the world by 1920.

Gearing

If you turn the left gear in the direction the arrow is pointing, which way will the right gear move? Draw an arrow to show your answer.

ANSWERS

Scrambled Groceries

FLOUR

BREAD

EGGS

MILK

SUGAR

CEREAL

RICE

Ambulance Amusement

The surgeon was the boy's mother.

Tot Ride

TOT RIDE=**DETROIT**

Gearing

Yarrrrrrr PIRATES

Sneaky

Can you find the fifteen pirate ships hidden in the letter grid? Look for:

3 SCHOONERS
5 BARQUES
7 SLOOPS

Hint: Use a marker to highlight each boat!

```
R S S P I R E N O O H C S E
E E L E U Q R A B S R L U P
N U O O A T P E L S O Q O B
O Q O H O O I O P O R O S A
O R P P O P O I P A L R A R
H A T L E P S H B S I P S Q
C B S P I R E N O O H C S U
S L O O P A E U Q R A B T E
```

Lazy Ammo

To find the silly answer to the question below, start at the letter marked with a dot. Collect every other letter until you reach the end. The trick is figuring out which way to travel around the circle!

What does a cannonball do when it isn't being fired?

Booty-ful!

This beautiful gem contains the names of several jewels and precious metals. See how many kinds you can form by using only letters that are attached to each other. Circle the ones in this list that you can find:

amber
gold
silver
diamond
ruby

emerald
sapphire
topaz
pearl

(Octagon gem puzzle with letters: A L D A / U R D I A / B E M E I A / Y E R O M / S V O M / I L N G / Z D)

Be Afraid

Pirate attacks were designed to make their victim's knees shake. Can you find four words that mean "to frighten" hidden in this grid? Take one letter from each column moving from left to right. Each letter can only be used once, so cross them off as you use them.

```
S L A C K
A H O R E
P C A I M
S A N R C
```

Avast!

"Davy Jones's Locker" is a sailor's term for the bottom of the ocean, especially meant as a grave for drowned sailors, lost treasure, and sunken ships. No one really knows where this term came from, but it was first used around 1750.

Easy Off?

Break the Number Substitution Code (1=A, 2=B, etc.) to read this riddle.

23-8-1-20   7-15-5-19   8-1   8-1   8-1

16-12-15-16?   1   16-9-18-1-20-5

12-1-21-7-8-9-14-7   8-9-19   8-5-1-4   15-6-6!

Avast!

The fictional Captain Hook was given many characteristics of the real Blackbeard!

EVERYTHING KIDS'

ANSWERS

Sneaky

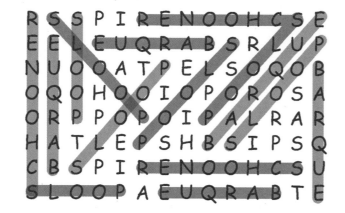

```
R S S P I R E N O O H C S E
E E L E U Q R A B S R L U P
N U O O A T P E L S O Q O B
O Q O H O O I O P O R O S A
O R P P O P O I P A L R A R
H A T L E P S H B S I P S Q
C B S P I R E N O O H C S U
S L O O P A E U Q R A B T E
```

Booty-ful!

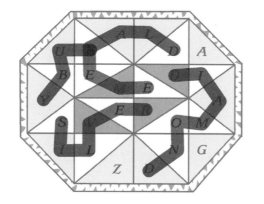

Lazy Ammo

Read counter-clockwise around the circle to find the answer: "It just looks round!"

Be Afraid

SCARE
ALARM
PANIC
SHOCK

Easy Off?

23-8-1-20 7-15-5-19 8-1 8-1 8-1
W H A T G O E S H A H A H A

16-12-15-16? 1 16-9-18-1-20-5
P L O P? A P I R A T E

12-1-21-7-8-9-14-7 8-9-19 8-5-1-4 15-6-6!
L A U G H I N G H I S H E A D O F F!

Four Fast Fixes

Choose words from the dark box that rhyme with each of the words in the sentences below. Write them on the lines provided. When you are finished, you will learn four things you can do to help save energy and resources! Hint: It helps to read each sentence aloud and slowly.

LOSE OATH STRIDES DOVE HAY CEASE DOVE VAPOR

_____

BURN COUGH BITES MEN VIEW WEAVE HAY TOMB

_____

FOOT PLANS TWIN DUH WEE-MICHAEL CHIN

_____

LEARN SCOFF DAUGHTER GLEN BLUSHING WREATH

_____

USE	OFF	SIDES	PAPER	OFF
LIGHTS	WHEN	YOU	TURN (2)	IN
LEAVE	PUT	ROOM	CANS	OF
PIECE	BOTH	THE	BIN	A
WATER				OF
BRUSHING	WHEN	TEETH	RECYCLE	A

Water Warning

If rain falls on an environment that has been contaminated (made dirty with chemicals) it won't be safe to drink. You can help prevent this! Figure out which two extra words appear over and over in the puzzle grid. Cross out all the extra words and read the remaining message!

CLEAN NEVER DRINK POUR CLEAN CHEMICALS DRINK LIKE CLEAN PAINT, DRINK PESTICIDES, CLEAN OR DRINK OIL CLEAN ON DRINK THE CLEAN GROUND. DRINK RAIN CLEAN CAN DRINK WASH CLEAN THEM DRINK DOWN CLEAN THE DRINK STORM CLEAN DRAIN DRINK OR CLEAN THROUGH DRINK THE CLEAN SOIL CLEAN INTO DRINK THE CLEAN WATER DRINK SUPPLY!

The Answer Is "Worms"!

What is the question? To find out, use the directions to cross out words from the grid. Read the remaining words from left to right and top to bottom!

Cross out words that...
...rhyme with TRASH
...have double vowels
...mean BIG

CLASH	MASSIVE	WHAT
SMALL	WOOD	HUGE
BOOK	WIGGLY	ENORMOUS
CREATURES	CAN	SKIING
SMASH	HELP	TURN
VEGGIE	VACUUM	WASTE
GASH	INTO	DASH
PRECIOUS	COLOSSAL	COMPOST

Great Idea!

There is a very simple way to save a lot of energy in your home. If you do, that means there is a lot more energy that can be used somewhere else! Break the Last-to-First Code to learn more.

ompactC luorescentf ightl ulbsb seu ne-o uarterq fo het lectricitye hatt a egularr ightl ulbb sesu.

ANSWERS

Four Fast Fixes

Use both sides of a piece of paper.

Turn off lights when you leave a room.

Put cans in the recycle bin.

Turn off water when brushing teeth.

Water Warning

~~CLEAN~~ NEVER ~~DRINK~~ POUR ~~CLEAN~~ CHEMICALS ~~DRINK~~
LIKE ~~CLEAN~~ PAINT, ~~DRINK~~ PESTICIDES, ~~CLEAN~~ OR
~~DRINK~~ OIL ~~CLEAN~~ ON ~~DRINK~~ THE ~~CLEAN~~ GROUND.
~~DRINK~~ RAIN ~~CLEAN~~ CAN ~~DRINK~~ WASH ~~CLEAN~~ THEM
~~DRINK~~ DOWN ~~CLEAN~~ THE ~~DRINK~~ STORM ~~CLEAN~~ DRAIN
~~DRINK~~ OR ~~CLEAN~~ THROUGH ~~DRINK~~ THE ~~CLEAN~~ SOIL
~~CLEAN~~ INTO ~~DRINK~~ THE ~~CLEAN~~ WATER ~~DRINK~~ SUPPLY!

The Answer Is "Worms"!

~~DASH~~	~~MASSIVE~~	WHAT
SMALL	~~WOOD~~	~~HUGE~~
~~BOOK~~	WIGGLY	~~ENORMOUS~~
CREATURES	CAN	~~SPRING~~
~~SMASH~~	HELP	TURN
VEGGIE	~~VACUUM~~	WASTE
~~DASH~~	INTO	~~DASH~~
PRECIOUS	~~COLOSSAL~~	COMPOST

Great Idea!

Compact fluorescent light bulbs use one-quarter of the electricity that a regular light bulb uses.

Facinating Fossils

Animals from the Past

Can you find the six differences between these two fossils?

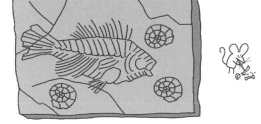

Words to Know

fossils:
Fossils are formed when the remains of a plant or animal become replaced with sediment containing materials like sand that eventually hardens into stone, leaving an image of the plant or animal that once was there.

Fossil Fractions

Look at the fraction below each blank. Pick the shape that shows that fraction, using these rules: the white part of each shape is empty; the shaded part of each shape is full. Write the letter of that shape on the line. When you are finished, you will have the answer to this riddle:

What do you call a fossil that doesn't ever want to work?

S   O   N   B

E   Y   A   Z   L

___ ___ ___ ___   ___ ___ ___ ___ ___
1/2 2/3 1/4 1/3   2/5 3/4 2/7 3/5 1/8

Find the Fossil

Dr. Pole has just had a new discovery named after him! Use the following clues to discover which fossil is the "Poleumita."

- The Poleumita does not have wings.
- The fossil to the left of Poleumita is a tooth.
- The Poleumita is not broken in half.
- The Poleumita has a spiral pattern.

EXTRA FUN: Read the letters with the fossils from bottom to top, and right to left, and you will find the answer to this riddle:

What do you call a petrified T. Rex?

How Do Scientists Know That Some Dinosaurs Were Professional Racers?

Cross out letters that appear more than five times in the letter grid. Read the remaining letters from left to right, and top to bottom.

```
T B G B H J G J E B J G M Y B G J F B J B O
J U M B J X N J M J D M B X X F M X M X O M
B M S X S G X B I B M M L J G M I G Z J G J
M G M J X J B M M B G X J M G M X J X B M E
D X G M D G X G J I M B M N X J B X O X J X
B M S X B X A M M X U M J M R X X M J T X G
J X G J M J M M B G X J J B X G J R M X B M
B G M J A X G X C X J K X G M J B X B M J S
```

ANSWERS

Animals from the Past

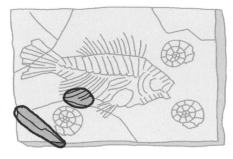 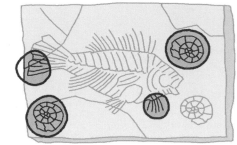

Fossil Fractions

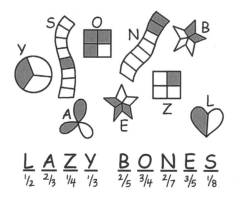

L A Z Y   B O N E S
1/2 2/3 1/4 1/3   2/5 3/4 2/7 3/5 1/8

How Do Scientists Know That Some Dinosaurs Were Professional Racers?

T B G B H J G J E B J G M Y B G J F B J B O
J U M B J X N J M J D M B X X F M X M X O M
B M S X S G X B I B M M L J G M I G Z J G J
M G M J X J B M M B G X J M G M X J X B M E
D X G M D G X G J I M B M N X J B X O X J X
B M S X B X A M M X U M J M R X X M J T X G
J X G J M J M M B G X J J B X G J R M X B M
B G M J A X G X C X J K X G M J B X B M J S

They found fossilized dinosaur tracks!

Find the Fossil

POLEUMITA

A petrified Tyrannosaurus is "A COLOSSAL FOSSIL!"

Planes, Trains, & Cars

Design a License Plate

You may have noticed that states sometimes change the designs of their license plates. A state may also change the "slogan" or words on its license plate.

Come up with your own slogans and designs for different states' license plates. When picking slogans, you can either be serious or goofy! The same goes for the design. On real license plates, often the colors will have something to do with the state's geography or its famous places, like green for a state that's known for all its forests. But this doesn't have to be true. You could draw a joke license plate with a picture of the motel you stayed at and a slogan like "The rain-soaked state," if it was raining while you were there.

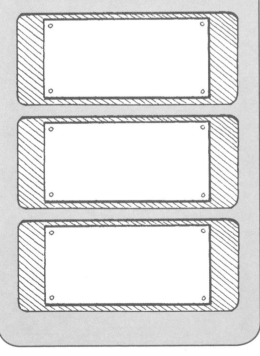

Beep Beep

The Dot family has spent the day at a giant craft fair. Now it's time to go home, but where is their car? Look around carefully —Papa Dot had it painted a special way, and even got a special license plate. Can you spot the Dots' car, and find the family a path to it?

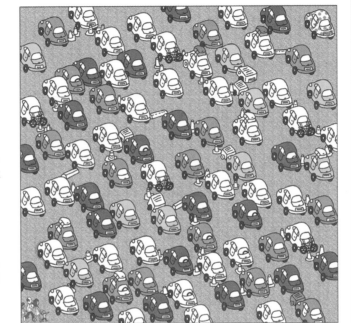

Who Parked Where?

Three cars are parked next to each other in a rest area. By reading the clues below, can you tell which people are going to get into which vehicle, the color of the vehicle, and what state they are from? HINT: Use the grid provided to help figure out the answers.

- The man with a dog is not in a silver truck and is not from New York.
- The blue vehicle is not from Maine.
- The family in the red vehicle is not from Maine or Ohio.
- The twin sisters are in a truck with a Maine license plate.
- The sports car is from New York.
- The van is not silver or red.

	vehicle	state	color
man with dog			
twin sisters			
family			

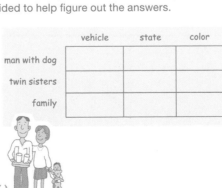

Word Search

In this word grid, see if you can find thirteen things you might see when driving along the coast. The words can go backward, forward, up, down, and diagonally.

BRIDGE
BUOY
FISHERMEN
KITES
LIFEGUARDS
LIGHTHOUSE
LOBSTER POT

ROWBOAT
SAILBOAT
SAND
SEAGULL
SURFERS
WAVES

```
S S S A I L B O A T S
L D E E G D I R B E L
O R R T S H E S V I L
B O E A I L L A G S L
S W S E U K W H A S U
T B H E L G T L S B G
E O Y T S H E Y H E A
R A S A O E A F O S E
P T N U H O R E I U S
O D S U R F E R S L B
T E F I S H E R M E N
```

EXTRA PUZZLE POINTS: After you have circled all the listed words, read the leftover letters from left to right, and top to bottom. You will find a popular tongue twister!

ANSWERS

Beep Beep

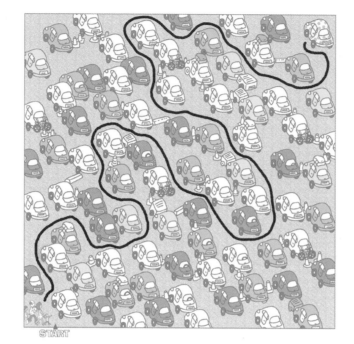

Word Search

Extra letters spell:
She sells seashells by the seashore.

Who Parked Where?

	vehicle	state	color
man with dog	van	Ohio	blue
twin sisters	truck	Maine	silver
family	sports car	New York	red

Gross & Gruesome

Spooky Spider

Don't you hate it when a spooky mutant monster spider gets between you and your home? Luckily, Josh knows the route. Can you find it?

start

finish

All spiders have 8 legs, but only a few have fangs.

Is that true or false?

NEW TO YOU

Recently, scientists discovered 40 new species of animals in a volcanic crater on the island of New Guinea. They include a frog with fangs, a fish that grunts, and a species of rat believed to be the biggest in the world. These animals have no fear of humans, having never seen us before!

Forgetful Dr. Frankenstein

Dr. Frankenstein is trying to build a monster, but he's so forgetful he can't find all the body parts. Can you find everything hidden in his lab?

- 2 sets of teeth
- 2 legs
- 2 hands
- 1 ear
- 2 hearts
- 2 fingers
- 5 eyeballs
- 2 noses

So Silly

These bugs are having a fun time. Want to join them? To join in the silly sayings, all you have to do is figure out the first letter.

__urple __arrots __lay __roudly

__low __nakes __lide __outh

__y __other __ixes __onkey __usic

__hildren __arefully __hoose __heese

__ossy __ugs __uild __arricades

Critter Chaos

Insects have some pretty amazing names. There are actually only 4 bug names here, but the words have been separated. Can you figure out which words go together to make proper names?

FLEA

MIMOSA

MAPLEWORM

PEA

GRAPE

WEBWORM

GREENSTRIPED

WEEVIL

BEETLE

ANSWERS

Spooky Spider

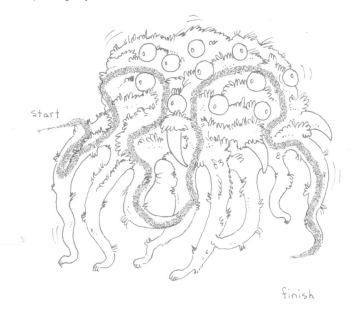

Riddle answer: Most spiders have fangs

Forgetful Dr. Frankenstein

So Silly
**Purple parrots play proudly
Slow snakes slide south
My mother mixes monkey music
Children carefully choose cheese
Bossy bugs build barricades**

Critter Chaos
**Grape Flea Beetle, Greenstriped Mapleworm,
Mimosa Webworm, Pea Weevil**

EEK!

Uh-Oh, Elevator

Some people hate riding in an elevator. They're afraid that it will fall while they are inside. If this sounds like you, beware—you have to ride an elevator in this puzzle! Each floor contains 1 word for you to find. Start at the bottom and go up 1 floor at a time. On each floor, you will be looking for a word that changes only 1 letter from the word below it. We have provided a clue for each floor to help you as you move up . . . and up . . . and up!

14th Floor: Past tense of shake
13th Floor: To photograph or film
12th Floor: To slide while seated
11th Floor: A large ladle
10th Floor: Type of sailboat
9th Floor: Embarrassing blunder
8th Floor: Flower of a plant
7th Floor: Dim light
6th Floor: Husband of a bride
5th Floor: Brush with a long handle
4th Floor: To think moodily
3rd Floor: Red liquid in our veins
2nd Floor: To cover with water
1st Floor: The bottom F L O O R .

14.	S H O O K S B O O M T
13.	S C O O L S H O O T I
12.	S H O O P S C O O T N
11.	H B O O R S C O O P T
10.	S L O O P C L O O P R
9.	S P O O R B L O O P E
8.	B L O O M L F O O D K
7.	G L O O M G D O O M H
6.	T R O O P G R O O M S
5.	C R O O P B R O O M Y
4.	B R O O D F T O O T U
3.	F L O O M B L O O D I
2.	F L O O D I M Y
1.	F L O O R D A R

Monster's Lair

There are 22 scary words hidden in this monster's lair. How quickly can you find them all? Use a highlighter to mark the words, then read the leftover letters from left to right and top to bottom to find a riddle!

AFRAID **CREEPY** **GROAN** **PANIC** **SPOOK**
ALARM **DREAD** **GROWL** **RATTLE** **SQUEAL**
BOO **EEK** **HOWL** **SCREAM** **THUD**
CACKLE **FEAR** **MOAN** **SHOCK** **TERROR**
CLANK **FRIGHT**

```
W H A C G R O W L T W
O G U L D A S Y E O U S U
R O R R E T F C R E E P Y H S
E D T O O M H R R K C E K A A O S
S Q U E A L U G A E R L E A M L O C N
R S H T N E R I I A ' S A E L W A I V K
K A T I N G Q R D M U N A O M R A C R
T O T E R S ? F A G R K H A F M I V E
Y B O T A R           D E N S T I
C O K P L O           D A E R D F
C O O U S E           P R R S E !
```

Batty for Fruit

Fruit bats use their keen sense of smell to find ripe rainforest fruit. By spitting out the seeds or dropping them as they fly through the forest, bats help new fruit trees to grow. Choose one of the dropped letters to add to each fruit. Then unscramble the letters and write the correct fruit names on the dotted lines.

1. I G

2. A N O M

3. A A N N A

G F B

1. _ _ _ _ _
2. _ _ _ _ _
3. _ _ _ _ _

ANSWERS

Uh-Oh, Elevator

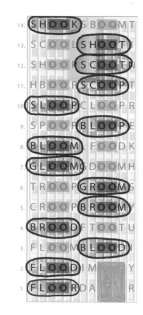

14. (SHOOK)SBOOMT
13. SCOOL(SHOOT)
12. SHOOR(SCOOT)N
11. HBOOR(SCOOP)T
10. (SLOOP)CLOOPR
9. SPOOR(BLOOP)E
8. (BLOOM)FOODK
7. (GLOOM)GDOOMH
6. TROOP(GROOMS)
5. CROOP(BROOM)Y
4. (BROOD)FTOOTU
3. FLOOM(BLOOD)I
2. (FLOOD)IMLY
1. (FLOOR)DAR

Monster's Lair

WHACGROWLTW
OGULDASYEOUSU
RORRETFCREEPYHS
EDTOOMHRRKCEKAAOS
SQUEALUGAERLEAMLOCN
RSHTNERIIA'SAELWAIVK
KATINGQRDMUNAOMRACR
TOTERS?FAGRKHAFMIVE
YBOTAR   DENSTI
COKPLO   DAERDF
COOUSE   PRRSE!

The extra letters read: What would you
use to measure a monster's living
quarters? A graveyard stick of course!

Batty for Fruit

G   F
  B

1. F I G
2. M A N G O
3. B A N A N A

Bon Appetit!

What do you call a giggling field of corn?
Laughing stalks.

What does Count Dracula use to cut his food?
A "stake" knife.

What kind of food is sick all the time?
Wheat germ.

When 2 eggs were placed in a blender, the first egg asked, "What's going on here?" What did the second egg say?
"Beats me."

How does bread get up in the morning?
It rises.

Why do melons rarely marry?
They "cantaloupe" (can't elope).

Knock knock!
Who's there?
Omelet.
Omelet who?
Om-e-let stronger than you think!

Knock knock!
Who's there?
Justin.
Justin who?
Justin time for dinner!

Fry It

Use the clues to make 10 words that rhyme with FRY. With a white pencil, circle these words in the frying pan grid.

Round dessert = __ __ __

Shed tears = __ __ __

A male = __ __ __

How come? = __ __ __

Soft breath = __ __ __ __

Stop living = __ __ __

Opposite of low = __ __ __ __

Neck clothing = __ __ __

To purchase = __ __ __

Wink with this = __ __ __

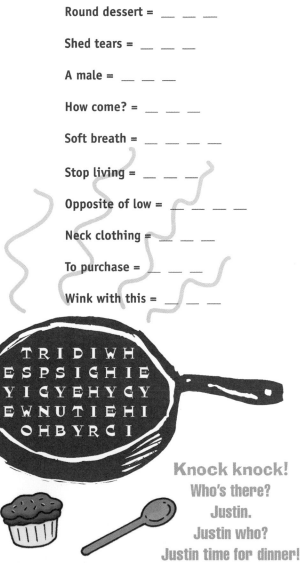

```
T R I D I W H
E S P S I C H I E
Y I C Y E H Y C Y
E W N U T I E H I
O H B Y R C I
```

Kid's Choice

When you are in a restaurant, what food do you like to order? See if you can find the 10 kid-favorite foods and beverages hidden in this puzzle. HINT: There's no word list, but we did leave you the waitress's order pad. Can you read her abbreviations?

```
Z I L T M A H T H S I M W I
I F K E H A T D N A E A I Z
D R G E W T E H T O S C R E
S E L O I V E R D C L A O S
C N O U D G O O C U T R A N
N C O H C T N U L E V O A H
C H E I N H O A W H C N I L
H F T S P A G H E T T I E C
A R E W O M U L D B A A E K
T I F U N B W E L Z T N H E
S E O N L U Y W Z A Y D T H
U S A T K R I I S G O C E N
R N I L E G P P A H O H T G
C H I C K E N N U G G E T S
T M S I F R S O M E T E H I
H I R A H C I T A M A S G T
G N P P L E M O N A D E E S
```

CK. NG.
HMB
H.D.
MACnCH

PZ
SPGH
F.F.

I. CRM
LMND
MLK

BLUE
YELLOW
LILAC

EVERYTHING KiDS.

ANSWERS

Fry It

T R I D I W H
E S P S I G H I E
Y I G Y E H Y G Y
E W N U T I E H I
O H B Y R C I

Round dessert = P I E   **Stop living =** D I E

Shed tears = C R Y   **Opposite of low =** H I G H

A male = G U Y   **Neck clothing =** T I E

How come? = W H Y   **To purchase =** B U Y

Soft breath = S I G H   **Wink with this =** E Y E

Kid's Choice

Z I L T M A H T H S I M W I
I F K E H A T D N A E A I Z
D R G E W T E H T O S C R E
S E L O I V E R D C L A O S
C N O U D G O O C U T R A N
C H E I N H O A W H C N I L
H F T S P A G H E T T I E C
A R E W O M U L D B A A E K
T I F U N B W E L Z T N H E
S E O N L U Y W Z A Y D T H
U S A T K R I I S G O C E N.
R N I L E G P P A H O H T G
C H I C K E N N U G G E T S
T M S I F R S O M E T E H I
H I R A H C I T A M A S G T
G N P P L E M O N A D E E S